Computational Capitalism

How AI Inequality Will Shape The Next Gilded Age

By

Alexander Grant

"What's not fully realized is that Moore's Law
was not the first paradigm to bring
exponential growth to computers. We had
electromechanical calculators, relay-based
computers, vacuum tubes, and transistors.
Every time one paradigm ran out of steam,
another took over."

--Ray Kurzweil

Alexander Grant

Table of Contents

Introduction

In the heart of Silicon Valley, a tale of two cities unfolds. On one side, tech moguls amass unprecedented wealth, their fortunes ballooning with each AI breakthrough. On the other, workers grapple with job insecurity and wage stagnation, their futures uncertain in an increasingly automated world. This stark contrast echoes a familiar narrative from America's past – the Gilded Age, where robber barons accumulated vast riches while the masses struggled.

Welcome to the era of computational capitalism, where artificial intelligence drives economic growth and shapes societal structures. But what exactly is computational capitalism? It's a system where AI and machine learning algorithms become the primary engines of wealth creation, often concentrating power in the hands of a few tech giants.

As we venture into this new landscape, we must confront a pressing question: How is AI reshaping our economy and exacerbating inequality? The centralization of AI technologies in the hands of a few corporations mirrors the monopolistic tendencies of the 19th century, creating modern-day "data barons" who wield enormous influence over our digital lives.

This book aims to unpack these complex dynamics, drawing parallels between our current technological revolution and historical patterns of wealth accumulation. By understanding the mechanisms of AI-driven inequality, we can better navigate the challenges ahead and work towards a more equitable future.

The stakes couldn't be higher. As AI continues to advance at breakneck speed, its impact on jobs, education, and social mobility grows exponentially. Without careful consideration and proactive measures, we risk sleepwalking into a new Gilded Age – one where the benefits of AI are concentrated among a privileged few, while the majority face increasing economic uncertainty.

It's time to spark a crucial conversation about the role of AI in shaping our society. By examining the ethical implications of AI development and deployment, we can forge a path that harnesses the potential of these technologies for the greater good. This book invites you to join this vital dialogue, equipping you with the knowledge and insights needed to become an active participant in shaping our collective future.

Alexander Grant

Chapter 1: The Dawn of Computational Capitalism

Defining Computational Capitalism

In today's fast-changing economy, "Computational Capitalism" isn't just a trendy phrase; it's an essential idea for grasping how technology is transforming our economic landscape. This concept highlights a major shift where advanced data analysis, machine learning, and automation blend with traditional capitalism. It helps us see how these technological advancements are changing how wealth is created and shared in our societies.

At the heart of computational capitalism is the idea that data has become a valuable resource. In the past, wealth came mostly from physical things like land, labor, and money. Now, we're living in a time when data is the new currency. Every click, swipe, and interaction produces a wealth of information, creating a goldmine for those who know how to use it. This change has sparked a revolution in business practices, as companies compete fiercely for the data that drives their decisions.

Algorithms play a vital role in computational capitalism. They are like the unseen forces guiding economic choices, influencing everything from what products we buy to job availability. These algorithms sift through enormous amounts of data to uncover insights, helping businesses optimize their operations and predict market trends more accurately than humans ever could. They decide what ads we see, what jobs are offered, and even who we connect with online. This has deep implications since these algorithms can reflect and even worsen existing inequalities, concentrating power among a select few who are tech-savvy.

Think about what this means for jobs. As AI becomes more capable of taking on tasks that used to require human workers, the job market is bound to change. Automation is ready to take over jobs across many fields, from manufacturing to service jobs. This unsettling reality raises important questions about the future of work. Who will reap the benefits of the efficiencies that automation brings? Will those who lose their jobs find new opportunities, or will they struggle with economic uncertainty?

The effects of computational capitalism reach beyond just the economy; they also touch on governance and society as a whole. Policymakers are facing the tough task of regulating technologies that change so quickly while trying to ensure fair distribution of resources. The algorithms that guide our daily lives often operate in a mysterious way, making them hard to understand and evaluate. This lack of clarity raises ethical questions about accountability and bias. For example, how can we make sure that AI systems don't continue existing biases in hiring or law enforcement?

Ownership of data and privacy issues add another layer of complexity to the landscape of computational capitalism. As companies gather and profit from consumer data, concerns about individual rights and protections grow louder. Balancing innovation with privacy is tricky, and finding that balance requires careful conversations among tech experts, ethicists, and policymakers. A pressing question remains: who should own the data that people generate? Should individuals have control over their personal information, or is it better left to corporations that can use it for profit?

By exploring the idea of computational capitalism, we start to see its effects on society. It's not just a technical change; it signals a shift in power dynamics, economic systems, and individual rights. The forces at work in this new environment are complicated and deserve our careful attention.

As we try to make sense of this complex world, it's crucial to support practices that encourage fairness and inclusion. The lessons from the Gilded Age remind us that unregulated capitalism can lead to glaring inequalities. We need to learn from the past and actively work towards a future where technology benefits everyone and doesn't just deepen existing divides.

In short, "Computational Capitalism" captures the spirit of a new economic era where technology, data, and wealth are closely linked. By understanding what drives this shift, we can start to address the ethical challenges and societal impacts that come with it. The ground is set for a deep look at the forces shaping our modern world as we strive to untangle the complexities of this new paradigm and discover ways to promote fairness and justice in an AI-driven society.

Technological Foundations

In the rapidly changing world of computational capitalism, technology is not just a backdrop; it's the main driver of this exciting era. Every day, breakthroughs in machine learning, automation, and data analysis are telling a story that transforms industries and changes the way we think about our economy. This story is fascinating, complex, and sometimes even a bit scary. The stakes are high because these technologies impact every part of our lives—from how businesses run to the nature of jobs, and even the fundamental ideas of fairness and justice.

At the frontlines of these changes is machine learning, which has completely changed how organizations can predict and understand trends. In the past, businesses typically relied on gut feelings and experience to guess what customers wanted and how markets would move. Now, thanks to machine learning, companies can sift through massive amounts of data to find patterns that would otherwise go unnoticed. Picture it as a brand-new kind of crystal ball, one based on solid data and analysis. Businesses can now foresee what customers will want and need with impressive accuracy, creating personalized experiences that feel almost magical. This ability not only boosts customer happiness but also helps companies run more smoothly, saving money and time.

However, this amazing technology does come with challenges. As machine learning algorithms become integral to decision-making, we face serious questions about bias, transparency, and accountability. These algorithms are designed by people and can unintentionally carry forward existing biases, especially in sensitive areas like hiring, law enforcement, and lending. For example, consider a hiring algorithm that favors candidates from specific backgrounds simply because it was trained on data that reflects past biases. The results can be significant, leading to ongoing inequality in workplaces and institutions. In this new environment, we must ask: who is held responsible when an algorithm leads to negative outcomes?

Automation is another key part of this technological framework, changing the job landscape in ways that are both thrilling and concerning. With machines taking over tasks that humans once did, the potential for greater productivity is huge. In manufacturing, for instance, production lines can run non-stop, creating products faster and with fewer mistakes. The service industry is also feeling the impact, with chatbots and virtual assistants stepping in to handle customer service tasks that used to need a human touch.

Yet, this surge in automation comes with significant effects on employment. As machines take over repetitive tasks, many workers find themselves without jobs. The fear of job loss is very real, putting livelihoods at risk and causing stress. The job market is starting to divide; those with advanced skills are thriving, taking advantage of new opportunities created by technology, while others, who lack the training or resources, struggle to keep up.

This situation reflects wider economic trends we've seen grow over recent decades, highlighting a widening skills gap. People who can adapt to the changing job landscape—by embracing technology and learning new skills— are rewarded with better-paying positions, while those who fall behind face stagnation.

This growing inequality not only impacts individual lives but also creates a cycle of economic disadvantage, as wealth increasingly gathers among those with access to education and opportunities.

At the core of this transformation is data analytics, the critical link that ties together machine learning and automation. In today's information age, data is often compared to oil—a resource of immense value. Businesses nowadays are swamped with data from all sorts of sources, including customer interactions, social media posts, and market trends. When used wisely, this data can empower organizations to make smart choices that help them stay ahead of their competitors. For example, a retail chain can analyze buying habits to manage stock better—making sure popular items are always available while reducing unsold products. This leads to happier customers and better profits.

On the flip side, relying on data analytics raises important questions about privacy and ethics. As companies gather and analyze large amounts of personal information, issues of consent and ownership come to light. Who owns the data generated by individuals, and how should it be used? Should companies have unrestricted access to consumer data, or should individuals have control over their own information? Finding a balance between using data for innovation and protecting personal privacy is a tricky but necessary task.

As we move further into this era of technological change, it's vital to consider the wider social implications. The balance of power in this new capitalist system is shifting; technology companies, with their vast data and advanced algorithms, are becoming major economic players. This centralization of power raises concerns about a few individuals holding too much influence. The potential for these companies to shape not just markets but also societal norms is significant, as they can guide consumer habits and public conversations in ways that may reinforce existing inequalities.

Additionally, the impact on governance is profound. Policymakers face the tough job of regulating technologies that evolve at lightning speed. The challenge isn't just about creating effective regulations but also about ensuring these rules lead to fair outcomes. The algorithms that drive economic decisions, often operating in a black box, need scrutiny to ensure they promote fairness and don't reinforce biases—an effort requiring teamwork from technologists, ethicists, and lawmakers.

The echoes of the Gilded Age are striking. Just like the industrial giants amassed wealth and power in the late 1800s, today's tech leaders are navigating a landscape that invites scrutiny and calls for oversight. History teaches us that unregulated capitalism can lead to glaring inequalities and social unrest. As we stand at this crossroads, the need to learn from the past and actively shape a future where technology serves everyone fairly has never been clearer.

As we look at the technological foundations of computational capitalism, we find a landscape full of promise but also complexity. The connections between machine learning, automation, and data analytics are changing how we live, work, and relate to each other. As we step into this next chapter of our economic journey, we must engage in thoughtful discussions about the ethical dilemmas, regulatory needs, and societal effects that come with these technological strides. By promoting inclusivity and fairness, we can navigate this new world together and aim for a future that benefits everyone.

Historical Parallels

The Gilded Age, a term introduced by Mark Twain, brings to mind images of vast fortunes accumulated at breakneck speed, standing in stark contrast to the harsh realities of poverty and social struggle. This period in the late 19th century was marked by rapid industrial growth, where innovation thrived and America emerged as a leading economic force. However, it was also a time when glaring inequalities and monopolistic practices grew rampant, leaving many people hungry for change. As we face a new economic era shaped by artificial intelligence and digital advancements, it's valuable to look back and find connections between the Gilded Age and our current age of computational capitalism.

In the Gilded Age, a small group of industrialists known as "robber barons" held tremendous power. Figures like John D. Rockefeller in oil and Andrew Carnegie in steel accumulated extraordinary wealth, often prioritizing profits over the well-being of their workers and customers. Their companies operated as monopolies, stifling competition and taking advantage of labor. The fallout from these practices went beyond just the economy; they left a society rife with tension as workers organized strikes and demanded the rights that they felt had been denied. Today, we see a similar pattern as new monopolies arise in the digital landscape, with tech giants like Amazon, Google, and Facebook exerting control over large parts of our economy and culture.

During the Gilded Age, technological advancements like the steam engine, the telegraph, and the railroad reshaped industries, changing how goods were transported and how people connected with one another. Fast forward to today, and we find ourselves at another crucial turning point, this time driven by data and artificial intelligence. The digital age is introducing transformative technologies that promise to make our lives easier and more efficient, much like the innovations of the past. But as we welcome these exciting changes, we need to be mindful of the impacts they can have on society, especially the inequalities they might worsen.

Just as wealth concentrated in the Gilded Age, we see a similar trend emerging today in the tech industry. The major players in Silicon Valley aren't just influencing the economy; they're affecting how we live our daily lives. The algorithms that control our online experiences, from the advertisements we encounter to the news we read, can create echo chambers that reinforce our existing views and widen divides. The monopolistic behaviors of today's tech titans echo those of the past, consolidating power in ways that can stifle competition and innovation while also increasing the gap between those with access to technology and those without.

The stark economic divides of the Gilded Age sparked a national dialogue about the need for reform. The Progressive Era that followed was characterized by widespread efforts to regulate industries, improve working conditions, and ensure the government acted in the public's interest rather than just benefiting the wealthy elite. The battle against corruption and the quest for social justice defined this time. Now, as we navigate the upheaval brought on by technology, we find ourselves at a similar crossroads. The rise of computational capitalism calls for a close examination of how technology is shaping our economy and our lives, urging us to ask pressing questions about governance, fairness, and accountability.

The labor movements of the Gilded Age, driven by desperation as workers faced dangerous conditions and meager wages, highlight the struggles of power dynamics. Organizations like the Knights of Labor and the American Federation of Labor emerged to demand rights and protections for workers. Today, we witness a revival of this fight as gig economy workers—often lacking traditional employment benefits—struggle for recognition and fair treatment in a technology-driven world. The challenges they face are complicated; the flexibility of gig work offers freedom, yet it comes at the cost of security and stability, a modern paradox that reflects the battles of the past.

Furthermore, just as the Gilded Age led to increased government regulation in response to corporate greed, today's tech landscape demands a solid governance structure. As artificial intelligence becomes a key player in decision-making across sectors, from healthcare to finance, the need for transparency and accountability is more important than ever. Policymakers must ensure these technologies do not fuel existing biases but instead promote fairness and inclusivity. This challenge resonates with the antitrust movements of the early 20th century, which aimed to break up monopolies and restore competition. In the realm of AI, we must advocate for regulatory frameworks that prevent power from concentrating and ensure that technological progress benefits everyone.

The recurring theme of inequality, evident in both the Gilded Age and our current digital era, highlights the need for proactive measures. History shows that without intervention, wealth tends to concentrate, leading to social unrest. This cycle often prompts public outcries, reminiscent of the labor strikes and protests that marked the late 1800s. As we confront rising concerns about privacy, algorithmic bias, and the digital divide today, we must heed the lessons of history. Our society stands at a critical juncture, where the choices we make about technology and its governance will determine whether we continue a system that serves a privileged few or create one that is fair and just for all.

In this reflection on history, we must strive for inclusivity as we navigate the challenges of our AI-driven world. The lessons from the past remind us that technological advancements aren't automatically beneficial; their effects depend on the values and structures we put in place. We should advocate for an approach to artificial intelligence that emphasizes ethical considerations, responsibility, and social equity. By doing this, we can ensure that the benefits of innovation are widely distributed, aligning with the democratic ideals that form the backbone of our society.

As we explore the connections between the Gilded Age and our present day, we uncover a story that resonates just as much today as it did over a hundred years ago. The struggles and achievements of those who came before us can light the way as we tackle the challenges posed by computational capitalism. Progress isn't a straightforward journey; it's a complex mix of victories and setbacks, where history's lessons can guide our future.

The urgency of this moment is clear. Just as past reform movements aimed to address the imbalances of their time, we are also called to action against modern inequities. Technology is evolving rapidly, and the choices we make today will have lasting impacts on future generations. Engaging in thoughtful discussions, pushing for fair practices, and holding powerful companies accountable are vital steps we need to take in order to shape a future that benefits everyone, not just the privileged few.

By acknowledging the repetitive patterns of inequality and the historical lessons that shape our present, we gain a deeper understanding of what's at stake. The rise of computational capitalism presents incredible opportunities, but it also brings challenges that require our collective focus and effort. History teaches us that unchecked power can lead to exploitation and social unrest. As we navigate the complexities of AI and its place in our economy, we must keep these lessons in mind and work toward a future that embraces fairness, inclusivity, and accountability.

The discussions around computational capitalism are not just academic; they touch our personal lives. As we journey through this technological transformation, we need to think about our roles as individuals, consumers, and citizens. Building a fairer future won't rely solely on policies and regulations; it will also need a commitment to ethical practices and a shared effort to ensure that technology serves humanity—rather than the other way around.

In the grand narrative of economic history, we find ourselves at a crucial moment where the insights of the past can illuminate the way forward. The Gilded Age offers both warnings and inspiration. As we reflect on how technology interacts with society, we must stay vigilant in our pursuit of a fair and just future. The road ahead will have its challenges, but it also presents a chance to redefine our relationship with technology and to create a new story—one that prioritizes the dignity and well-being of every individual as we confidently move into the future.

Chapter 2: The Centralization of AI Power

Monopolization Dynamics

The rise of artificial intelligence is changing the way industries work and opening up a heated discussion about the concentration of power in the hands of a few big companies. Today, the world of AI is largely influenced by a small number of organizations that hold incredible sway over large parts of our economy and daily lives. This monopolization isn't just a natural result of market trends; it's a strategic move reflecting larger patterns in capitalism and governance.

When we look more closely at the monopolization happening in the AI field, we see that the impacts go beyond just profits and market shares. The growing centralization of AI power affects competition, innovation, and the very fabric of our social and economic systems. For example, we can see how the current landscape features a few dominant players—technology giants that seem to have taken over the market. Companies like Google, Amazon, Microsoft, and Facebook have not only gained immense wealth but have also gathered enormous amounts of data, which is crucial for developing AI technologies.

In this situation, data is the new oil. It's the essential resource that powers machine learning and drives AI advancements. The more data a company can collect, the more effective its AI tools become. This creates a cycle: as these companies innovate and develop better technologies, they secure their positions even further, making it harder for smaller businesses and startups to compete. These smaller players often find themselves at a serious disadvantage, trying to go up against the massive benefits that the large tech companies possess.

The barriers to entering the AI industry are daunting. New companies not only need technical know-how but also have to navigate a complicated web of regulations and financial demands. The expenses involved in building the necessary infrastructure, hiring the right talent, and gathering data are often overwhelming. Many hopeful innovators face challenges that seem impossible to overcome, which effectively keeps them out of a field that is quickly becoming a key part of modern economies. This trend towards monopolization can stifle competition and limit innovation, as a lack of diverse viewpoints can lead to similar technologies that may not meet everyone's needs.

Additionally, this buildup of power has serious consequences for how we govern ourselves. When a small number of corporations control the tools that shape industries and influence consumer behavior, they can sway public policy and legislative decisions. This situation can create what some experts call "regulatory capture," where the interests of these mighty entities start to overshadow the needs and rights of ordinary people. Policymakers often find themselves stuck between wanting to promote innovation and needing to ensure fair competition. As a result, we often see regulations that favor established companies, making it even tougher for newcomers to make their mark.

The global impact of this monopolization is just as critical. As AI technologies spread across different sectors, countries that don't have strong AI capabilities may find themselves at a serious disadvantage. The race for AI dominance isn't just about economic strength; it's also tied to national security and global power dynamics. Countries that don't invest in AI research and development risk becoming reliant on the technology of others, surrendering control over important parts of their economies and societies.

In this light, the monopolization of AI can widen existing global inequalities. Countries that are already struggling economically may find it hard to be part of the

AI revolution, positioning them as consumers rather than innovators. This sets up a two-tier global system, where a select few reap the benefits of AI while many others are left out in the cold.

We also cannot ignore the ethical issues that come with this concentration of AI power. As companies collect more data and create advanced AI tools, they gain the ability to influence social behavior and alter decision-making processes. The algorithms behind our online experiences are often complex and hidden, and their effects can be significant. Concerns around bias, privacy, and surveillance grow in a world where a small number of corporations can control what information we see and how it's shared.

The potential for abuse of power is especially alarming in AI-driven systems that impact important areas like hiring and law enforcement. If we don't keep a close eye on this, the monopolization of AI could result in a future where a privileged few not only hold the wealth but also dictate how society operates. This scenario is reminiscent of the Gilded Age, a time known for stark economic divides and unchecked corporate power.

As we think about these monopolization dynamics, it's vital to look for ways to create a more balanced AI landscape. Policymakers, tech experts, and the public need to come together to advocate for fair access to AI technologies and meaningful competition. Pushing for regulation, transparency, and accountability in the AI sector is not just an academic concern; it's a crucial step to ensure that the benefits of AI reach everyone rather than being hoarded by a wealthy few.

The journey toward fairer AI practices won't be easy, but it calls for open conversations, creative solutions, and a dedication to inclusivity. The stakes are high, and the choices we make today will impact our societies for years to come. If we aim for a future where technology benefits everyone and not just the elite, we can move toward a more just world—one where the promise of AI is fulfilled for all people.

In short, the monopolization dynamics seen in the AI sector remind us why we must stay alert and take action. The effects of concentrated power are deep and complex, influencing competition, governance, and global fairness. It's up to everyone involved to recognize these challenges and actively work toward an environment where innovation thrives for the many, not just the privileged few.

As we continue to explore the intricacies of AI and its effects, it's crucial to keep our eyes on the bigger picture: building a system that empowers individuals, encourages competition, and ultimately leads to a fairer, more prosperous future for all. The road ahead may be filled with obstacles, but with teamwork and determination, we can create a landscape where AI is a tool for collective progress, not a means of reinforcing inequality.

Barriers to Access

As the sun sets on the exciting advancements brought about by artificial intelligence, a tough reality comes into view: not everyone will benefit from this technological wave. The buzz around AI often ignores the significant barriers that stand in the way of fair access to its tools and knowledge. These obstacles take many shapes, and recognizing them is crucial for building a future where AI empowers everyone and doesn't deepen existing inequalities.

When we discuss these barriers, we first need to face the issue of economic disparities. The financial landscape for developing AI is quite intimidating, especially for startups and small businesses that lack the financial clout of their larger competitors. The costs tied up in AI development can be overwhelming. From gathering the massive datasets that drive machine learning algorithms to the computing power needed to develop high-performance models, the expenses can quickly run into millions. This reality creates a significant divide between those who can afford to thrive in the AI sector and those who can't.

For new businesses, finding funding feels like wandering through a minefield. Many entrepreneurs come equipped with brilliant ideas, yet they often struggle to land the investment they need. Venture capitalists, drawn in by the allure of AI, typically favor established companies with a history of success over promising newcomers who might not have the same track record. As a result, a harmful cycle emerges: established firms keep gathering resources while innovative startups struggle under financial pressure. This leads to a market that lacks diversity, silencing new voices and limiting the potential for groundbreaking discoveries.

Take, for example, a small tech startup trying to develop an AI-based healthcare solution. With tight budgets, they face the double hurdle of gathering the data they need while competing against industry giants that already have vast datasets and strong partnerships. While larger companies can dedicate significant funds to research and development, the startup might be barely scraping by to cover their basic expenses. This stark financial difference creates an uneven playing field, stifling competition and innovation—not just for the startups themselves, but also for consumers who ultimately benefit from a variety of offerings.

Now, as we shift our focus to educational barriers, another layer of complexity emerges that prevents equitable access to AI. The gap in skills within the workforce is a pressing concern, particularly regarding AI training and educational programs. While interest in AI careers is growing, many aspiring tech professionals find themselves lacking the foundational skills needed to succeed in this fast-changing field. Adding to the challenge is the limited access to quality education and training, especially for underrepresented groups.

The truth is, access to AI education is not evenly spread. People from marginalized backgrounds often face systemic challenges that make it harder for them to acquire the skills needed for AI roles. Traditional education routes—whether through colleges or specialized training—can be prohibitively expensive and out of reach for many. As a result, countless potential innovators are left waiting in the wings, their talents untapped and their ideas unrealized.

Let's illustrate this with the differences between urban and rural educational institutions. In cities, students often have access to specialized programs, internships, and networking opportunities that link them to the AI industry. In contrast, students in rural areas may find themselves in schools without the resources to offer advanced technology courses, leaving them unprepared for a future in AI. This educational divide perpetuates inequality and reinforces an environment where diverse thoughts and experiences struggle to be heard.

Additionally, the lack of representation in AI fields can create blind spots in technology development. When a narrow group of people shapes the algorithms and datasets powering AI systems, the risk of bias and exclusion rises significantly. For instance, facial recognition technology has been criticized for its inaccuracies in identifying individuals from different racial and ethnic backgrounds—issues that arise from training data that doesn't adequately represent those groups. To tackle these problems, it's vital to prioritize inclusivity in AI education, ensuring that people from all backgrounds have equal chances to contribute.

We also need to highlight the geographic and infrastructural barriers that worsen the inequities in accessing AI technology. Around the world, there are significant differences in technological infrastructure, especially in developing regions where many people still lack dependable internet and computing resources. Rural and economically challenged areas often find themselves stuck in a digital divide, where the absence of basic tech resources deepens existing inequalities.

Imagine talented data scientists living in a remote village without reliable internet. Despite their skills, they cannot access the same resources or training as their urban counterparts. Without a stable internet connection, they struggle to download essential datasets, participate in online courses, or collaborate with peers in real time. This isolation holds them back and stifles the growth of local talent. Consequently, innovation becomes centered in urban areas, continuing the cycle where geographical location dictates access and opportunity.

In many developing countries, governments are often unable to keep pace with rapid technological advancements. Investments in infrastructure and education frequently fall short, leaving communities behind. The challenge is not just about accessing technology but also about fostering a strong environment that supports innovation. When regions lack basic infrastructure—like reliable internet, computing facilities, or educational opportunities—they are effectively shut out of the AI revolution. The consequences of this exclusion are significant, as entire communities miss out on the economic benefits that AI initiatives could bring.

As we navigate these complex barriers, it's clear that the path to fair access to AI technology is filled with challenges. Economic, educational, and infrastructural disparities come together to undermine the potential for widespread participation and innovation in the AI sector. Addressing these issues requires a comprehensive approach—one that not only recognizes these barriers but also actively works to break them down.

Collaboration is essential for creating a more inclusive AI environment. Governments, educational institutions, and private organizations need to join forces to invest in initiatives that expand access to education and resources for underrepresented groups. By establishing scholarships, mentorship programs, and community training opportunities, we can begin to bridge the gap and empower individuals from all walks of life to engage in the AI landscape.

Additionally, policymakers must prioritize building technological infrastructure in underserved areas. Investing in broadband access and digital literacy programs can help level the playing field, allowing communities to tap into the power of AI and contribute to its growth. By championing inclusivity and accessibility, we can create a rich variety of voices that will help shape the future of AI technology.

The urgency of addressing these barriers is undeniable. As AI continues to transform our world, the effects of exclusion will only become more significant. The demand for innovation and diverse perspectives is greater than ever as society grapples with the ethical implications of AI. When only a select few are positioned to steer AI technology's development, we risk creating systems that reinforce existing biases and inequalities.

It's our shared responsibility to ensure that the advantages of AI aren't reserved for a privileged few but are distributed across all of humanity. The future of AI should be one where the contributions of individuals from all backgrounds are recognized and celebrated. By breaking down access barriers, we can create a fairer and more just world—where AI stands as a powerful force for positive change instead of a driver of inequality.

As we approach this new era, the choices we make today will shape the future of AI for the generations to come. We must push for policies that promote inclusivity, empower aspiring tech professionals, and dismantle the barriers that have historically sidelined marginalized voices. By doing this, we can unlock the full potential of AI and ensure it becomes a symbol of hope for a future defined by fairness and opportunity for everyone. The journey toward a more inclusive AI landscape may be challenging, but with determination and teamwork, we can create a path forward that truly reflects the diversity of human experience.

The stakes are enormous, but the opportunities are limitless. If we dedicate ourselves to this mission, we can change the story surrounding AI from one of exclusivity and domination to one of shared opportunity and progress. Together, we can build a world where everyone—regardless of their background, where they live, or how much money they have—has the chance to join in the AI revolution, enjoying its benefits and helping to shape its future for the good of society as a whole.

Global Implications

In the vast world of global power dynamics, artificial intelligence has stepped into the spotlight as a major player, influencing not just technology but the very heart of international relations and economic strategies. As we witness this new era of human progress, one thing is clear: the concentration of AI power in the hands of a few countries and corporations is reshaping the geopolitical landscape in profound and complex ways.

At the center of this shift is a race for AI dominance, similar to the Cold War arms race, but now it's about algorithms and data instead of missiles and warheads. Countries are investing billions in AI research and infrastructure while competing fiercely to gain the upper hand in this crucial area. The stakes are high, with the quest for AI leadership affecting everything from trade deals to national security. Governments understand that being able to harness and control AI technologies is tied closely to economic success, military strength, and global influence. This realization drives policies aimed at boosting domestic AI development while limiting competition from abroad.

Consider the United States and China—two giant competitors in the AI field whose rivalry has grown into a complex contest. The U.S. is pushing its tech companies for groundbreaking solutions, while China is pouring resources into state-backed AI projects. This battle isn't just about having the best technology; it's a strategic fight for soft power where the victor could set the rules and standards for AI's growth and use around the world.

But the implications don't stop at national borders. Countries that lag behind in this tech race risk losing their edge in global trade. As AI becomes more vital to industries like agriculture, manufacturing, and finance, those who can't keep up will struggle. Nations with strong AI capabilities can use their tech assets to secure advantageous trade deals, monopolize essential resources, and influence global markets. In contrast, those without such capabilities may find themselves marginalized, fighting to stay relevant in an AI-driven economy.

Additionally, the concentration of AI power raises significant national security concerns. The rise of AI technologies has changed traditional ideas about warfare and intelligence. Cybersecurity threats, autonomous weapons, and surveillance systems are all enhanced by AI, making it crucial for nations to view AI not just as a tool for economic gain but as a key part of their defense strategies. This shift leads countries to rethink their security approaches, often resulting in increased military budgets for AI research and development.

In this landscape, the risk of an arms race fueled by AI technologies looms large. A new type of arms race is taking shape, one focused not just on physical weapons but also on the ability to control and use advanced algorithms for decision-making in warfare. The potential consequences for international security are enormous. With AI systems in the mix, conflicts could escalate much faster. The likelihood of mistakes increases when decisions made by AI aren't fully understood or controlled by humans. If an AI can react quicker than human leaders, it might cause unintended and dangerous outcomes—something countries need to navigate with extreme caution.

As we ponder these geopolitical challenges, the need for countries to work together becomes crystal clear. The effects of AI monopolization aren't limited to individual nations or companies; they spill over borders, impacting global trade, security, and the well-being of societies. This isn't just a matter of who controls AI; it's a crucial conversation about how we can all ensure that its development is beneficial for humanity as a whole.

In this complex web of global relations, the demand for discussions between nations becomes louder. Countries need to collaborate to share knowledge, set standards, and create ethical guidelines that govern AI technologies. A united approach can help reduce risks tied to AI centralization while fostering inclusivity and fairness on a worldwide scale. Just as we've seen with other pressing issues like climate change and public health, the challenges we face are interconnected, needing joint solutions that go beyond national interests.

One of the most urgent topics in this discussion is the creation of ethical AI standards that protect human rights and dignity. The risk of bias and discrimination in AI algorithms threatens not only individual rights but also social stability. Nations must join forces to develop a framework ensuring AI technologies are created and used responsibly, guarding against abuses that could emerge from unchecked power.

Global cooperation is also vital for economic partnerships. Countries that work together on AI projects can share resources, talent, and knowledge, driving innovation. By forming joint ventures and collaborations, nations can benefit from shared insights and lessen the risks tied to technological monopolies. This spirit of cooperation can contribute to a fairer landscape, where the benefits of AI are spread more evenly among countries and communities.

However, reaching this level of collaboration is not without its hurdles. National interests often collide, leading to protective policies that hinder cooperation. Countries might hesitate to share vital technologies or best practices, fearing it could compromise their competitive advantage. Overcoming this reluctance requires a change in mindset—one that sees our global society's interconnectedness and recognizes our shared responsibility to ensure AI is a force for good.

The need for action is urgent. As AI technologies continue to advance and affect every part of our lives, the implications of their concentration will deepen. History tells us that when power is held by a select few, it usually results in systemic inequalities that are hard to dismantle. The monopolization of AI could worsen existing disparities, leaving vulnerable populations more marginalized in a world that is increasingly automated.

To carve out a better future, we must support initiatives that promote fair access to AI technologies worldwide. This includes investing in educational programs that equip people from diverse backgrounds with the skills they need to thrive in an AI-focused economy. It also involves promoting entrepreneurship and innovation in regions that have traditionally been left out of the tech scene. By breaking down barriers to access, we can create a global talent pool that reflects the richness of human experience.

Moreover, policymakers need to focus on international regulations that tackle the monopolistic tendencies in the AI sector. Establishing guidelines that encourage competition and prevent a small number of corporations from consolidating power is crucial to ensuring that the benefits of AI technologies are fairly distributed. By emphasizing ethical considerations and human rights in AI development, we can lay the groundwork for a future that upholds our shared values while harnessing the remarkable potential of this technology.

Chapter 3: Economic Implications of AI Domination

Wealth Accumulation Mechanisms

In today's fast-changing tech world, few things spark as much discussion and concern as artificial intelligence. While AI has incredible potential to drive progress in different areas, it also plays a significant role in creating wealth that tends to benefit only a small group of people. This tendency to concentrate wealth is strikingly similar to what we saw during the Gilded Age, a time known for its extreme economic inequality and monopolistic practices.

To understand how this wealth accumulation happens, we first need to look at data's unique role in the digital age. People often say that data is the new oil—a valuable resource that, when properly refined and used, can lead to huge profits. Tech giants have mastered this resource like no one else, mainly because of their AI capabilities. Companies like Amazon, Google, and Facebook have not only gathered enormous amounts of data but have also created complex algorithms that take advantage of this data to generate value.

Take Amazon, for example. It started out as a simple online bookstore and has now become a global retail giant. Its success isn't just about convenience; it comes from using algorithms to optimize pricing, manage inventory automatically, and predict customer behavior with impressive accuracy. By analyzing customer data, Amazon not only personalizes shopping experiences but also consistently stays ahead of the competition. This data-focused approach highlights a key way that wealth is accumulated in the AI era: it creates barriers that make it difficult for new companies to enter the market.

In a similar vein, Google has changed how we find and share information, using its vast collection of user data to improve its search algorithms and advertising strategies. Google's search engine, a fundamental part of the internet, works on a pay-per-click system that rewards businesses for getting visibility. Unfortunately, this system usually favors larger companies that can afford to bid high for ad placements, further deepening existing economic divides. The more data Google collects, the more powerful its algorithms become, allowing it to tighten its grip on the advertising market.

Meanwhile, Facebook has transformed social interaction into a money-making machine, using user-generated content to power its advertising platform. The algorithms on Facebook focus on engagement, which creates a cycle where content that gets more interaction is prioritized. This approach not only boosts popular, sensational content creators but also sidelines smaller voices that struggle to get noticed. The concentration of wealth in advertising revenue creates a feedback loop that benefits established brands and influencers, pushing newer creators to the sidelines.

Venture capital also plays a big role in widening the wealth gap through its support of AI-driven startups. These funds often favor companies that use AI solutions, neglecting those that might offer more equitable or socially beneficial services. As a result, we see an ecosystem where a small number of companies receive most of the investment, allowing them to dominate their markets. The wealth generated from these businesses often stays within a narrow circle of investors and executives, further concentrating financial power and reinforcing inequalities.

The current situation also raises important questions about who owns the data behind these algorithms. The truth is often murky, but it usually benefits corporations more than individuals. Users willingly share their data for free services, but this exchange often lacks clarity. As algorithms become smarter, the potential for misuse increases. Companies can use this data to predict behavior, influence decisions, and ultimately extract even more value from their customers. This exploitation is reminiscent of labor practices from the Gilded Age, where workers were often seen as mere tools for generating wealth for their bosses without receiving a fair slice of the profits.

The connection between AI and wealth accumulation also brings up urgent concerns about regulations. Current antitrust laws, designed to prevent monopolies, seem ill-suited to tackle the unique challenges that AI technologies present. Our legal system, built for the industrial age, struggles to understand the complexities of a digital economy where data serves as both a commodity and a crucial asset. Policymakers need to figure out how to adapt laws to ensure fair competition, encourage innovation, and protect consumers in a world dominated by algorithms.

As wealth continues to flow into the hands of a few, the consequences of such inequality go beyond mere numbers. A society where wealth is so unevenly distributed can lead to social unrest and erode trust in institutions. When the average person feels like the system is rigged in favor of the wealthy, it can result in growing disappointment in democracy itself. The Gilded Age serves as a historical reminder of how unchecked wealth can fracture society, and the lessons from that time need to guide our approach to the AI-driven future.

The potential for wealth accumulation in the AI era is enormous, but it raises pressing ethical questions about fairness and equity. As we navigate this new landscape, we must consider both the economic impacts and the wider social consequences. Achieving a fairer distribution of wealth will require collective effort and innovative policy solutions to tackle the unique challenges posed by AI. Whether through establishing data ownership rights, improving regulatory frameworks, or encouraging diverse business models, there's a critical need to ensure that the advantages of AI are shared widely, rather than hoarded by a privileged few.

By examining the ways wealth is being generated in the age of AI, we uncover the complex relationships between technology, data, and economic power. This ever-changing environment calls for diligence, creativity, and thoughtfulness as we work to shape a future that embraces technological progress while prioritizing fairness and justice. The key question is: how can we make sure that the benefits of AI do not replicate the inequalities of the past but instead help build a more inclusive and just society? Tackling this challenge will require a societal commitment to creating an environment where innovation serves the greater good rather than simply reinforcing existing divides.

Labor Market Polarization

As the digital clock ticks away, marking each second and moving us closer to a future shaped by artificial intelligence, the impact of this technological evolution is becoming increasingly clear in the job market. The rise of smart systems is shaking up how we work, creating a sharp divide between high-skill, high-wage jobs and low-skill, low-wage positions. This division is more than just a passing trend; it's a fundamental change in our economy that is slowly eroding the middle class.

The numbers tell a compelling story. A report from the McKinsey Global Institute predicts that by 2030, around 375 million workers around the world might need to switch careers due to the rise of automation and AI. That's a huge shift that will change the types of jobs available and who can access them. As jobs for middle-income workers dwindle, the need for specialized roles in fields like technology, engineering, and data science is on the rise, while low-income service jobs are becoming more common. For instance, the Bureau of Labor Statistics expects healthcare support roles to grow by 22% and personal care aide positions to increase by 20% in the next decade. These jobs often come with high turnover rates and little stability, highlighting the growing demand for low-skill positions.

This divide has serious consequences for workers everywhere. Many find themselves in a precarious balancing act, trying to secure a stable job while living in an economy that increasingly rewards only those with advanced skills. As traditional industries automate and streamline operations, skilled workers often find themselves in a privileged position, while those stuck in low-wage jobs face significant insecurity. The reality is that job security is becoming more of a luxury than a guarantee. Gone are the days when one could expect to build a career in manufacturing or middle management over many years.

Looking closely at the labor market's changes, it's clear that the skills gap is widening. Employers are on the lookout for workers who can embrace new technologies and processes, leaving behind those who don't have the right training or education. Today's jobs often require specialized skills, yet access to education and training is not the same for everyone. This creates a situation where those who already have advantages can thrive, while individuals from lower-income backgrounds struggle to catch up.

It's urgent that we focus on reskilling workers. They need to have the right skills to succeed in a world increasingly influenced by

AI. Both companies and governments need to step up and create access to training programs that help workers adapt to these changes. Unfortunately, there is often a gap between what policies aim to achieve and what the workforce really needs. Many training programs are slow to adapt and are based on outdated practices that don't reflect the fast-evolving job market.

Beyond the statistics, the personal stories behind these numbers reveal the true impact of labor market polarization. Take Sarah, for example. She was an assembly line worker at a manufacturing plant that recently automated much of its operations. After two decades on the job, she found herself at a crossroads when the plant announced layoffs. The skills she had worked hard to develop over the years were suddenly useless. With limited access to reskilling options and bills piling up, Sarah had to settle for a low-skill job as a cashier. Unfortunately, her story is not unique; many workers find themselves in similar situations, caught off guard by technological advancements that leave them behind.

Then there's Jamal, a young software developer working in a thriving tech hub. He represents the other side of this job market divide. With a degree in computer science and a talent for coding, he has jumped into the high demand for skilled tech workers. However, even with his success, Jamal feels the pressure of his situation. The tech industry is always changing, and he knows that keeping his skills updated is not just a good idea; it's a must if he wants to keep his job. The constant need to learn and stay ahead in such a competitive field can be a heavy burden for workers like him.

These contrasting stories illustrate the harsh realities of labor market polarization. While Jamal may flourish in an environment that values his skills, Sarah faces growing challenges in a world that no longer sees her past experience as valuable. These different paths affect more than just individual lives; they also impact family stability, community structures, and social connections.

The situation with benefits is equally troubling. In the past, many workers enjoyed steady jobs that came with health care, retirement plans, and paid time off. Now, with the rise of gig economy jobs and contract work, these benefits are often out of reach. Workers in low-wage jobs frequently lack essential health care coverage, while those in the tech field often feel pressured to work longer hours without any job security. The decline of benefits not only affects individual well-being but also weakens the social fabric, as more people grapple with economic uncertainty.

Given this landscape, the need to tackle skill mismatches is urgent. Employers, educators, and policymakers must come together to create opportunities for lifelong learning. This means rethinking curriculums, adding practical training, and providing support systems that help workers transition into new roles. The challenge is not just in devising effective programs, but also in ensuring that everyone has equal access to these opportunities.

As we reflect on the polarization of the labor market, we must understand that the economic effects go beyond job loss and stagnant wages. When a significant number of people are stuck in low-wage, low-skill jobs with little chance of improvement, it can lead to rising tensions in society. Economic inequality creates frustration, and as the divide between the wealthy and the poor widens, we risk losing social cohesion and trust in our institutions.

Some might believe that the market will sort itself out and that the invisible hand of capitalism will create new jobs to replace the ones that have disappeared. However, this perspective oversimplifies the issue. The speed of technological change is outpacing the labor market's ability to adjust. The narrative about a workforce changing for the better due to innovation is often clouded by the harsh reality of displacement and instability for many workers.

As we think about what comes next, it's clear that addressing labor market polarization is as much a moral issue as it is an economic one. We must ensure that the future of work is inclusive, giving everyone a chance at meaningful employment and the chance to flourish. It's up to all of us—businesses, educators, and policymakers—to work towards building an economy that values every worker and recognizes the dignity of their contributions.

In this age driven by AI, the stakes are incredibly high. The choices we make today will shape the job market of tomorrow. If we don't take action to close the skills gap, support reskilling efforts, and ensure fair access to opportunities, we risk creating a system that benefits only a select few while leaving the majority behind. The decision lies with us: to create a future where technology empowers everyone or to allow it to deepen existing inequalities and widen the gap in our society.

As we navigate through these complex challenges, it's important to remember that the forces impacting our labor market are powerful and multifaceted. The experiences of individuals like Sarah and Jamal remind us that behind every statistic are real lives affected by the sweeping changes around us. It's our shared responsibility to make sure these changes lead to a fairer and more equitable future for all.

Economic Inequality Metrics

In the world of economics, numbers and figures tell stories of struggle, hope, and, unfortunately, inequality. As we find ourselves in a moment where artificial intelligence is driving innovation while also deepening the gap between the rich and the poor, understanding economic inequality metrics is more crucial than ever.

At the center of this conversation is the Gini coefficient—a well-known measure used to assess income inequality. This number ranges from 0 to 1, where 0 means everyone has the same income, and 1 means one person holds all the wealth while everyone else has none. While the Gini coefficient offers a way to visualize our economic situation, it begs the question: what does it really tell us about our society?

As artificial intelligence changes the way we work, we're seeing a major shift in how wealth is shared. Instead of being spread out, wealth is becoming more concentrated. A recent study from the Institute for Policy Studies reveals that the richest 1% of Americans own more than 15 times the wealth of the bottom half of the population. This shocking figure paints a picture of a society where the wealthy are not just getting richer; they are becoming powerful figures, overshadowing a growing population of people who are struggling.

If we look at the Gini coefficient for the United States, we notice it's been climbing steadily since the 1970s. Back in 1970, it was around 0.391, but recent data shows it has risen to about 0.488. This increase isn't just a number; it represents real challenges for millions of Americans. The growth of AI is a major player in this trend, as automation and efficiency primarily benefit those at the top of the wealth ladder.

However, the Gini coefficient isn't the only number we should pay attention to. Its shortcomings become clear when we examine different income brackets. For instance, while the top 10% of earners have seen their wages rise significantly, the middle class often struggles with stagnant or even declining incomes. This gap leads us to wonder if traditional metrics truly reflect the changing dynamics of wealth distribution.

When we look at graphs showing wealth distribution, they tell a vivid story of the widening divide between the ultra-wealthy and everyone else. These charts often reveal a striking imbalance, where the wealthy continue to thrive while those at the bottom fight just to get by. It raises an important question: how do we connect these statistics to the everyday experiences of individuals who feel left behind as AI continues to develop?

Worldwide studies have highlighted these shifts in wealth, largely driven by the rise of AI technology. The Brookings Institution found that jobs requiring routine manual or cognitive tasks are disappearing at an alarming pace. This trend raises serious concerns about the future for marginalized communities—those already facing challenges in economic mobility. As job opportunities shrink and the paths to advancement become harder to navigate, entire communities risk being trapped in cycles of poverty, with few options to escape.

A clear example of this can be seen in the retail sector, which has been transformed by AI. With automated checkouts and smart inventory systems becoming the norm, many low-skill jobs have disappeared, disproportionately affecting those from lower-income backgrounds. The National Employment Law Project highlights this issue, showing that low-wage workers are sinking further into economic hardship, struggling to compete with the efficiency of AI technologies.

It's vital to understand that traditional measures like the Gini coefficient fail to capture the real experiences of these individuals. Economic inequality isn't just a statistic; it shows up in health disparities, challenges in education, and the bleak outlook for future generations. As we dig into these issues, we should ask ourselves: are our current measures enough to tackle the complexities of inequality driven by AI?

We are at a crucial turning point that calls for a fresh look at the metrics used to measure economic inequality. The traditional indicators often miss the full picture of challenges posed by AI. We need new metrics that consider the unique struggles of the workforce in this fast-changing technological landscape.

Imagine a metric that not only looks at income but also examines job security, access to education, and opportunities for personal growth. A comprehensive approach like this would give us a clearer view of economic well-being, especially for those on the lower end of the income scale. By focusing on the many dimensions of inequality, we can start to understand the complex realities faced by individuals and communities impacted by these changes.

Additionally, we must think about how these metrics influence public policy. When policymakers focus solely on these statistics, they can get drawn into a narrow narrative that might not address the root causes of inequality.

The need for a more holistic approach is urgent. Policymakers need the right tools to make informed decisions that create effective solutions to combat disparities caused by AI.

The impact on social mobility is concerning. A study from the Pew Research Center shows that children born into low-income families are less likely to climb the economic ladder than their wealthier counterparts. As AI continues to reshape the job market, it is marginalized communities that suffer the most. If these trends continue, we risk raising a generation of individuals who not only struggle to find stable work but also lack access to the resources needed for upward mobility.

Tackling these disparities requires immediate action. One potential solution is the idea of universal basic income (UBI)—a policy that has sparked much discussion in recent years. By providing a guaranteed income, UBI could serve as a safety net for those whose jobs become obsolete due to AI. Supporters argue that this could empower people to seek education and training, fostering a more skilled workforce ready for the demands of the modern economy.

Alongside UBI, a fairer taxation system aimed at wealth gained from AI could be key to addressing economic disparities. This system would make sure that those who gain the most from technological advancements contribute their fair share. The funds raised could be used to support education and training programs, helping to build a more equitable society.

Moreover, ensuring equal access to education and technology is crucial for paving the way to success. As AI becomes more integrated into our lives, we must prioritize educational investments that build critical thinking, creativity, and adaptability—skills that are increasingly important in a tech-driven world. This effort requires collaboration between governments, schools, and businesses to make sure everyone, regardless of their background, has the chance to thrive.

As we explore the complexities of economic inequality metrics, it's clear that our current tools are lacking. The narrative of progress that comes with technological advancements must be balanced with a commitment to fairness and inclusion. By adopting new measures for inequality, supporting progressive policies like UBI and fair taxation, and investing in education, we can pave the way for a future where AI is a source of empowerment rather than oppression.

The path ahead is filled with challenges, but it's a journey worth taking. The choices we make now will shape the economic landscape for generations. Let's choose wisely and strive for a society that respects the dignity and potential of every person, ensuring that the benefits of technology are shared widely and fairly. Only then can we begin to tackle the complexities of economic inequality in the age of AI, building a world where everyone has a seat at the table and opportunities abound for all.

Chapter 4: AI and the Transformation of Labor

Automation and Job Displacement

As we step into a new era filled with rapid technological changes, one of the most important discussions we need to have is about automation and how it impacts jobs. The rise of artificial intelligence (AI) is a bit of a double-edged sword; it brings incredible efficiency, productivity, and innovation but also poses a real threat to jobs in many different areas. This change is not just about technology moving forward; it's also about how our economy and society are transforming.

To really grasp the scale of job loss caused by automation, we need to look at which industries are most at risk. A report from the McKinsey Global Institute highlights that about 60% of all jobs could see at least a third of their tasks automated by 2030. That's a staggering number and it gives us a clear view of the changes coming to the job market. Industries like manufacturing, retail, and transportation are particularly vulnerable because their repetitive tasks can easily be handed over to machines. For example, assembly line jobs, which have been a backbone of manufacturing for years, are now increasingly being taken over by robots that can work faster and more accurately than humans.

The retail space is experiencing a similar upheaval. The boom of e-commerce has changed how we shop, making many traditional stores less relevant. Self-checkout kiosks and online shopping have become commonplace, leading to numerous store closures and job losses. Take Sears, for example. Once a giant in retail, the company has faced a steep decline in sales and a significant reduction in its workforce as it struggles to compete with online rivals that use advanced algorithms to predict what shoppers want and manage their stock.

Transportation is also going through its own revolution, especially with the rise of self-driving cars. Companies like Tesla and Waymo are pushing hard to make autonomous vehicles a reality, aiming for a future where we might not need human drivers at all. This shift could spell trouble for millions of people working in trucking and ride-sharing, with a report from the American Trucking Associations estimating that about 3.5 million truck drivers in the U.S. could be at risk because of this technology. The consequences could be severe, with entire communities built around these jobs facing economic challenges and uncertainty as the need for human drivers fades away.

But the effects of automation go beyond just job loss. There are serious social implications to consider. As more people find themselves out of work or stuck in low-paying jobs, issues like income inequality and economic disenfranchisement grow more pronounced. The World Economic Forum notes that the richest 10% of the global population owns 82% of the wealth, highlighting the widening gap between the wealthy and everyone else. As automation picks up speed, this gap may only get larger, with the advantages of AI concentrating in the hands of a few while many struggle to get by.

The emotional impact of losing a job is also something we can't ignore. For many, a job means more than just a paycheck; it's a big part of their identity and purpose. Losing work can lead to feelings of worthlessness, depression, and anxiety. The American Psychological Association has found connections between unemployment and various mental health issues, including higher rates of substance abuse and suicide. As the job market keeps changing, we must think about how these shifts affect the mental well-being of workers facing displacement.

Some people argue that while automation may take away certain jobs, it also creates new ones. The idea is that as technology progresses, our workforce must adapt. Yes, new roles will come up as old ones disappear, but the transition isn't always smooth. The skills needed for these new jobs often look very different from those used in jobs that are being phased out. For instance, while there's a growing demand for data analysts and AI specialists, there's not much need for clerks and assembly line workers anymore. The real challenge lies in helping the existing workforce learn new skills to meet these evolving demands.

For many, the idea of picking up new skills can feel overwhelming. Imagine a factory worker who has spent years mastering their craft. Suddenly, they're told they need to retrain for a job that requires knowledge in coding or data analysis. It can feel intimidating and make them question their ability to navigate this new path. So, how can we support these individuals during this transition? Schools, government programs, and private companies need to work together to create training programs that help workers acquire the skills they need for the changing job market.

We need to take proactive steps to lessen the negative effects of automation on workers. As we look to the future, it's crucial that we put policies in place to help those most at risk of losing their jobs. Governments should think about social safety nets that provide financial support and retraining options for affected workers. The idea of universal basic income has gained attention recently as a possible way to give people the financial stability they need while they look for new opportunities. While this concept is still up for debate, it shows how urgent it is to deal with the challenges that automation brings.

On top of that, businesses that benefit from automation need to recognize their role in supporting the communities they operate in. Companies should invest in training programs that help their employees stay relevant as the job landscape changes. By encouraging a culture of ongoing learning, organizations can empower their workers to adapt and succeed as technology evolves.

The impact of automation on jobs is something we can't turn a blind eye to. The rapid rise of AI is changing job roles and calling for immediate responses from society. As industries undergo these major changes, we all need to advocate for fair practices that prioritize the well-being of workers. We must come together to find innovative solutions that help individuals navigate this new job landscape, ensuring that the benefits of AI and automation are shared widely, not just concentrated among a select few. The future of work is upon us, and it's up to all of us to shape it into one that is inclusive, fair, and just.

The Gig Economy 2.0

The gig economy has changed a lot in recent years. What once started as a way for people to find flexible work has turned into a complicated system that offers some benefits but also comes with its own set of challenges. This new phase, often referred to as "Gig Economy 2.0," is heavily influenced by artificial intelligence and the digital platforms that utilize it. Unlike the earlier days when people simply offered their services as freelancers, now, technology plays a major role in how work is assigned, how workers are assessed, how they are paid, and how they are treated.

At the heart of Gig Economy 2.0 is a shift from straightforward freelance jobs to a more complex environment driven by technology and data. Companies such as Uber, TaskRabbit, and Upwork have transformed the working world by using algorithms to control almost every part of gig work, from which jobs are available to how payments are made. These platforms rely on advanced AI to match workers with tasks, judge their performance, and set prices based on what's happening in the market. Unfortunately, this means that gig workers often find themselves at the mercy of hidden algorithms that prioritize profit and efficiency over their rights and job security.

The way employers and workers interact has been completely altered by algorithmic management, but not always in a good way. The algorithms that run these platforms can be confusing, leaving gig workers to deal with a maze of rules that can change with little warning. This lack of clarity can create a feeling of insecurity, as workers face the unpredictability that comes with gig jobs. For example, a driver for a ride-sharing service might see their earnings swing wildly based on demand, surge pricing, and customer ratings. Often, these workers have little recourse when they feel treated unfairly, as their livelihoods depend on a system that values numbers over human experience.

The uncertain nature of gig work is a real concern. Unlike traditional employees, gig workers usually don't have basic benefits like health insurance, paid time off, or retirement plans. This absence of support can create serious financial stress, especially during tough economic times or personal challenges. Take the story of Maria, a single mother juggling multiple gig jobs to make ends meet. Without health benefits, she often finds herself choosing between her child's medical needs and her own, which leads to delays in care for both. Plus, Maria's income isn't steady; one week she might earn enough to get by, while the next she could struggle to find enough gigs to pay her bills. This constant instability adds to her stress and anxiety, especially with the pressure to maintain good performance ratings to secure more job opportunities.

Many gig workers feel stuck in a tough position: they appreciate the flexibility that gig work provides, but they also crave the security and benefits that come with traditional jobs. The feeling of being disposable heightens when considering how platforms manage workers. If a gig worker receives low ratings from customers, they risk being removed from the platform entirely, often without any explanation or warning. The fallout from such a decision can be severe, throwing a person into financial instability in an instant.

Beyond the emotional and financial difficulties, the structure of the gig economy can also reinforce systemic inequalities. The algorithms that govern gig work can reflect and even worsen existing biases, making it harder for marginalized groups to access opportunities. Research has shown that job platforms may favor workers based on certain demographic traits—like location or favorable customer ratings—over others. This means that individuals from underrepresented backgrounds or those with limited access to technology may struggle to find gig work. Ironically, the very tools intended to make the job market more efficient can create barriers that keep those already facing hardships from entering the field.

Still, while gig work may sometimes feel like a never-ending treadmill, there are paths to change and collective action. As workers begin to recognize their collective strength, movements advocating for gig workers' rights are gaining traction. Organizations focusing on collective bargaining and pushing for policy changes are shining a light of hope for those seeking better working conditions. These groups aim to change the conversation around gig work, pushing for regulations that ensure basic protections and benefits for all workers, no matter their employment status.

Successful advocacy efforts are popping up globally, showing that workers can come together and demand fair treatment. For instance, in California, the passing of Assembly Bill 5 aimed to extend labor protections to gig workers by reclassifying them as employees instead of independent contractors. Although the law faced resistance from major gig companies, it sparked important conversations about gig workers' rights and their need for protections. This ongoing dialogue emphasizes the growing recognition of gig work as a legitimate form of employment that deserves fair treatment.

Another vital part of the advocacy effort is the demand for transparency in how algorithms make decisions. As gig workers increasingly rely on platforms that use AI to control their work lives, it's crucial to hold these companies accountable. Advocates are calling for clearer guidelines on how algorithms function, how workers are assessed, and what criteria determine job assignments. Collaboration among workers, policymakers, and tech companies is necessary to create an environment where gig work can flourish without compromising the rights of those involved.

The journey ahead may be filled with obstacles, but there is hope for positive change. Workers are stepping up by forming unions, advocating for their rights, and using social media to spread the word. As more people become aware of the challenges facing gig workers, there's a growing understanding of the complexities of this new economy and the urgent need for reform.

Alongside advocacy, there's a pressing need for businesses that benefit from gig work to recognize their ethical responsibility to support their workforce. Companies should not only focus on making profits but also consider how their practices affect the communities they serve. By investing in training programs, healthcare access, and other forms of support, these businesses can help build a more sustainable gig economy that values the contributions of its workers.

As we think about the future of work in this ever-changing landscape, we must recognize the unique challenges posed by Gig Economy 2.0. While AI has the potential to reshape labor dynamics, it also raises ethical questions that need to be addressed. We need to shift the conversation surrounding gig work from one of individualism to one of community and solidarity. By fostering a sense of shared responsibility, we can work toward a gig economy that meets the needs of consumers while also honoring the rights and dignity of gig workers.

This transformation won't happen overnight. However, through collective effort and increased awareness, we can lay the groundwork for a fairer gig economy—a space where workers are empowered, treated with respect, and provided with the benefits and protections that should come with any job. The gig economy is not just a passing trend; it's an important part of our labor landscape. Recognizing and addressing its complexities is vital to ensuring that the future of work reflects our shared values of fairness, transparency, and dignity for everyone.

Skill Gap and Education

As we find ourselves on the edge of major technological changes, one big problem stands out: the growing gap between what schools teach and what companies really need. This disconnect risks leaving many people behind as automation and artificial intelligence sweep through industries faster than ever. The truth is clear—many school programs are outdated and don't give students the skills they need to succeed in a tech-driven economy. This isn't just an academic oversight; it's a serious issue that calls for urgent and united action.

Looking at today's educational system, the picture isn't very bright. Many schools still stick to old teaching methods that were created for a different time. In classrooms around the world, students are often stuck memorizing facts and taking standardized tests, while outside those walls, everything is changing rapidly. Skills that were once considered essential, like typing or data entry, are now becoming obsolete as technology takes over those tasks.

Take the tech industry, for example. It's leading the way in innovation and change. Jobs that need advanced coding skills, data analysis, and knowledge of artificial intelligence are thriving, yet there's a big gap in the number of candidates who have these skills. Colleges and vocational schools are usually slow to change their programs to match the needs of the job market. This mismatch not only impacts fresh graduates trying to enter the workforce but also affects current employees who see their skills quickly becoming outdated.

For instance, the demand for AI-related positions—like machine learning engineers, data scientists, and AI ethics specialists—has surged, but educational institutions haven't been able to keep up in producing enough qualified candidates. Many new graduates, excited to start their careers, often discover they aren't well-prepared for the jobs they want. And this problem extends beyond just the tech industry; fields like healthcare, finance, and manufacturing are facing similar issues. Each of these industries is changing, driven by technological advances that need a new set of skills not covered in today's education.

The consequences are alarming. As the skill gap grows wider, companies struggle to find qualified workers, and individuals face the harsh reality of unemployment or underemployment. This cycle not only slows down economic growth but also worsens issues of inequality. Those without access to quality education or who can't afford to retrain are hit hardest, creating a larger divide between the fortunate and the less fortunate in the job market.

This brings up an urgent question: what changes do we need to make to close this expanding skill gap? The solution lies in a complete overhaul of how we think about education and vocational training. We must start teaching subjects like AI literacy, coding, and critical thinking in schools as early as possible. These skills shouldn't be limited to specialized schools or advanced degree programs; instead, they should be part of the core curriculum from the start.

Countries like Finland and Singapore have made impressive progress in this area. Finland has developed an education system that values creativity, teamwork, and problem-solving, while Singapore focuses on continuous learning and flexibility, keeping its workforce competitive amid change. We should study these models and adapt them to fit the unique needs of different areas and industries. By investing in training for teachers and providing the right resources, we can make sure that educators are ready to teach these crucial skills effectively.

Additionally, promoting lifelong learning for adults is vital. In a world where change is constant, education shouldn't just stop in early life. Adults need opportunities to gain new skills throughout their careers. This means creating training programs that are accessible and affordable for a diverse workforce. Online courses, community colleges, and corporate training can play a big role in making this happen, offering flexible and relevant paths for learning.

The success of these changes will be boosted by collaboration among different groups—schools, businesses, and policymakers. It's crucial that these players come together to create an education system that responds to the needs of the job market. Companies should take an active role in connecting with schools to share what skills they need and help shape curricula. This partnership can take many forms, from internships and apprenticeships to guest lectures and mentorship.

Examples from around the world show the effectiveness of such collaborations. In Germany, for instance, the dual education system combines classroom learning with hands-on training in workplaces. This approach allows students to gain practical experience while they are still in school, making them highly employable when they graduate. Companies also benefit, as they can train potential employees to match their specific needs.

Moreover, policymakers play a key role in creating an environment that encourages educational reform. Laws that support educational innovation, workforce development, and investments in training can greatly enhance the effectiveness of these reforms. Policymakers also need to ensure that marginalized communities have access to these opportunities, helping to bridge the gap for people who have been overlooked in the past.

Understanding the complex relationship between education and the job market is essential as we tackle the skill gap. It's not just about improving educational results; it's also about reshaping the future of work itself. Looking forward, we must cultivate a culture of adaptability and resilience—one that prepares individuals not only for today's jobs but also equips them with the skills to face the unknown challenges of tomorrow.

As we think about the future, we need to take action—not just as educators and lawmakers, but as a society that values equal access to learning and opportunity. To tackle this pressing issue, we must engage in meaningful conversations about the nature of work and the skills needed to thrive in a world that's changing rapidly. It's up to us to ensure that education evolves alongside technological advancements, creating pathways for everyone to succeed.

In this digital era, where the lines between work and learning are increasingly blurred, it's vital to recognize the importance of soft skills as well as technical knowledge. Skills like critical thinking, emotional intelligence, adaptability, and teamwork are crucial in a constantly changing job market. Schools must prioritize these abilities, preparing students not just for specific careers but also for the challenges they will face in an interconnected and dynamic world.

The road ahead won't be easy. Resistance to change, budget issues, and established interests can slow progress. But the potential benefits are too great to overlook. By addressing the skill gap and reforming our educational systems, we can create an inclusive job market that empowers individuals and communities. This is an investment in our shared future—a future where technology acts as a tool for empowerment rather than a barrier to opportunity.

In the face of rapid technological change, the skill gap brings both challenges and opportunities. It pushes us to rethink how we approach education, work, and their connection. Together, we can shape a future where everyone has the skills and opportunities needed to thrive, creating a fair and resilient job market for generations to come. As we navigate this complicated landscape, let's commit to advocating for educational reform, supporting lifelong learning, and promoting collaboration among all parties involved. The urgency of this mission is clear, as the power of technology is transforming our world faster than ever. It's time to rise to the challenge and ensure that no one gets left behind in the pursuit of progress.

Chapter 5: Political Power and AI

AI in Governance

The rise of artificial intelligence has sparked a significant change in how governments operate, offering exciting new ways to improve public services and decision-making processes. Around the world, governments are increasingly tapping into AI to tackle urgent issues, streamline their operations, and engage citizens in fresh and meaningful ways. Whether through predictive analytics that track public health trends or algorithms that help distribute resources more efficiently, AI is transforming governance in deep and sometimes surprising ways.

We can find many examples that highlight how AI is enhancing government efficiency. Take Estonia, for instance. This country is well-known for its digital approach to governance, and it uses AI to make public service delivery smoother. The Estonian government has employed machine learning algorithms to handle taxes and manage social benefits quickly and accurately. This not only cuts down on bureaucratic delays but also allows civil servants to devote more time to complex tasks that need human understanding and empathy. Estonia's approach shows how

AI can boost efficiency while also improving the overall experience for citizens by reducing wait times and making services more accessible.

Meanwhile, in Los Angeles, AI is being used for predictive policing, analyzing crime patterns to allocate police resources more effectively. The idea is not to violate civil rights but to proactively prevent crime. By using advanced algorithms to sift through vast amounts of data, law enforcement can pinpoint areas where crime is more likely to occur, allowing them to send officers to those hotspots. Still, while we celebrate these advancements, it's crucial to tackle the ethical issues that come with such technology. The risk of biased algorithms is a significant concern, threatening to undermine the promise of AI. If the data used to train these systems reflects existing biases, the algorithms could unintentionally reinforce systemic inequalities. In Los Angeles, critics have pointed out that predictive policing often unfairly targets marginalized communities, potentially deepening disparities instead of addressing them.

Another example that highlights the complex nature of AI in governance is Singapore's smart city initiatives. The government has rolled out AI technologies to enhance urban planning, traffic management, and environmental sustainability. By collecting and analyzing real-time data, Singapore is creating an infrastructure that better meets the needs of its citizens. However, this progress comes with a catch: increased surveillance. The extensive data gathering needed for these improvements raises serious questions about privacy and individual rights. Residents might feel as though they are being constantly monitored in the name of enhancing their quality of life, leading to growing unease about the balance between security and personal freedom.

The impact of AI on governance goes beyond just making things more efficient or allocating resources better; it touches on accountability and transparency. As we shift decision-making from human hands to algorithms, we have to ask: who is responsible for the outcomes these systems produce? When mistakes happen or injustices occur as a result of automated decisions, who is held accountable? This isn't just an abstract question; it's a real issue that deserves serious attention.

AI systems can often be like "black boxes," operating without clear reasoning. If a government uses an algorithm that denies services to a citizen without explanation, that person may find it very challenging to contest the decision. This lack of transparency is concerning, especially when we consider the potential for discrimination in algorithmic decision-making. If data sets are created without proper checks for bias, the results can reinforce existing inequalities, which goes against the very principles of democratic governance.

Addressing these ethical challenges makes human oversight incredibly important. While AI can analyze data faster and in larger volumes than humans, it doesn't possess the moral judgment that comes with human decision-making. So, it's vital to develop systems that ensure accountability. Some places are starting to recognize the value of having human checks in the decision-making process, blending human insight with the capabilities of AI to prevent possible injustices. This mixed approach aims to take advantage of AI's benefits while protecting against its drawbacks.

Legal and ethical guidelines for using AI in governance are still being developed. As governments explore ways to encourage innovation, they also need to create strong frameworks that prioritize civic responsibility. The General Data Protection Regulation (GDPR) in the European Union is a step in the right direction, focusing on the need for transparency and user consent in data collection. However, there's still a lot of work to do in creating comprehensive legal structures governing AI's role in public decision-making, ensuring that citizens maintain control over their data and the effects of algorithm-driven choices.

Moreover, getting the public involved is key to shaping policies on AI in governance. Citizen participation should go beyond just watching from the sidelines; it should include actively discussing AI technologies. This means educating people about what AI means for their lives and encouraging conversations about the values we want to uphold as a society. Without this involvement, AI could end up serving the interests of a few rather than benefiting everyone, undermining the democratic ideals that governance aims to uphold.

The challenges AI presents in governance can be addressed, but they require teamwork among many different groups—policymakers, technologists, ethicists, and the public. By working together to create frameworks that emphasize accountability and transparency, we can harness the potential of AI while protecting democratic values. As we navigate this new landscape, it's essential to stay alert to the ethical ramifications and strive for a future where AI is a tool for fairness and justice, not a source of division and inequality.

When we look closely at contemporary examples, we see that AI is more than just a technical tool; it holds the power to reshape governance itself. Its ability to improve efficiency and engage citizens is matched by the ethical challenges it brings. The conversation around AI in governance must continue, focusing on responsible innovation that respects the rights and needs of all citizens. The promise of AI in this field lies in our collective choices about how we use it. As we step into this digital era, the decisions we make now will have lasting effects for future generations.

Influence and Manipulation

As the sun sets over the digital world, casting long shadows across the political landscape, we find ourselves facing a powerful force that has seeped into the heart of our democratic processes: artificial intelligence. With its ability to sift through vast amounts of data and predict outcomes, AI has become both a tool for boosting civic engagement and a means of controlling the public. However, lurking beneath this dual nature is a troubling reality where misinformation and the misuse of algorithms can twist the very essence of democracy.

At the center of this manipulation is the spread of misinformation, which has flourished in our social media-driven age. The

2016 United States presidential election stands as a stark reminder of how AI technologies can be used to influence public opinion. During this heated election cycle, research showed that an alarming number of false narratives circulated on platforms like Facebook and Twitter, reaching millions before they could be disproven. These misleading stories often tapped into existing fears and divisions within society, creating confusion that ultimately swayed voter behavior.

One particularly deceitful tactic seen during the election was the use of advanced targeting algorithms. These algorithms were crafted to deliver custom content to specific groups, but they were manipulated to spread misleading messages to those who were more vulnerable. By playing on the psychological profiles of users, campaigns could create messages that struck a chord with their fears and hopes, often sacrificing factual accuracy in the process. This turned AI into a tool for division, sowing distrust among citizens and weakening the very institutions designed to uphold democratic values.

The fallout from AI-driven misinformation was also evident in the Brexit referendum in the United Kingdom. The Leave campaign skillfully employed data analytics to target voters with personalized messages that tapped into their emotions and misconceptions. Ads that played on fears about immigration and the economy flooded social media, drowning out factual discussions. Ultimately, the outcome of the referendum was less about informed choices and more about emotional manipulation, raising serious questions about the integrity of the democratic process.

As we dig deeper into these disinformation campaigns, we discover another potent weapon in the manipulation toolbox: surveillance technologies. The rise of AI-powered surveillance has blurred the lines between safety and personal freedoms, creating a chilling effect on civil liberties. Both governments and corporations have used these technologies to monitor dissent and suppress free expression, raising urgent ethical concerns about privacy and accountability.

Picture this: an activist group organizes a peaceful protest against government policies. In a world dominated by AI surveillance, every step they take is tracked, recorded, and analyzed. Facial recognition systems identify participants, while algorithms predict potential flashpoints for unrest. This overwhelming level of scrutiny not only intimidates activists but also fosters a climate of fear that stifles civic engagement. The right to protest, a cornerstone of democracy, becomes powerless under the relentless gaze of AI.

The ethical questions surrounding surveillance technology extend beyond government actions. Businesses, too, have started to infringe on civil liberties by using AI to monitor customer behavior and predict preferences. While companies argue that these practices are essential for enhancing services, they often overlook the potential for misuse. When the line between engaging customers and invasive surveillance blurs, individuals are left wondering about their privacy rights in a world increasingly ruled by algorithms.

At the heart of these issues is the widening gap in societal divisions. AI-driven platforms, motivated by profit, often prioritize engagement over truth. The algorithms that determine what content users see are designed to maximize clicks and interactions, accidentally creating echo chambers that reinforce existing beliefs and biases. This is especially noticeable on social media, where users are constantly fed information that aligns with their views, further deepening polarization.

The impact of this polarization is significant. As people retreat into their ideological corners, chances for meaningful conversations shrink. Instead of engaging with differing opinions, individuals get trapped in a loop of confirmation bias, where opposing voices are drowned out by a chorus of agreement. The result is a divided society, unable to bridge the gaps that separate us, making it increasingly difficult to tackle the pressing issues we all face.

To illustrate this, let's look at how algorithmic biases shape political discussions. Research has shown that certain groups are more likely to encounter extreme or misleading content because algorithms favor sensationalism over accuracy. This distorted representation not only skews public perception but also affects the political landscape, influencing everything from election results to policy choices. As a society, we need to take a hard look at the consequences of these biases, acknowledging that the very technologies created to inform us can also mislead us.

In light of these challenges, the need for a united response becomes clear. Protecting democratic values in the age of AI requires a multifaceted effort involving policymakers, tech developers, and the public. First and foremost, transparency is vital. Platforms must be held accountable for the algorithms they use, with clear guidelines about how content is curated and spread. Without transparency, citizens are left to navigate a murky digital world, often unaware of the forces shaping their thoughts and beliefs.

Additionally, promoting digital literacy is key to fighting misinformation and manipulation. Teaching people about how AI works and the biases that can emerge in algorithmic decision-making empowers individuals to critically assess the information they come across. By giving people the tools to separate fact from fiction, we can begin to rebuild trust in our democratic institutions.

As we navigate this new landscape, advocating for policies that prioritize ethical AI development is crucial. This includes creating regulations governing the use of AI in political campaigns and on social media platforms. By introducing guidelines that ban deceptive practices and mandate transparency in data collection, we can build a political environment that is less prone to manipulation.

Moreover, fostering conversations and partnerships between various stakeholders is essential for creating a fair digital ecosystem. Bringing together tech developers, ethicists, and civil society to discuss the ethical implications of AI can lead to responsible practices and innovative solutions to the challenges we face. Together, we can strive for a future where technology serves the public good rather than undermines it.

The intersection of political power and AI offers both promise and peril. As we confront the troubling aspects of influence and manipulation, we must recognize the responsibility that comes with this powerful technology. By pushing for transparency, enhancing digital literacy, and promoting ethical practices, we can reclaim the narrative and ensure that AI is used for the greater good. In this digital age, the decisions we make today will shape the political landscape for years to come, reminding us that the integrity of democracy rests in our hands.

Regulatory Challenges

As the sun rises on the exciting world of artificial intelligence, it shines a light on the incredible opportunities these technologies bring, while also revealing the unclear waters of regulation that lie beneath. With AI evolving at a breakneck speed, lawmakers are struggling to keep up. The big question is: how can we create a set of rules that are flexible and effective enough to handle the complex challenges that AI brings? In this new era, old regulatory methods often seem outdated, struggling to keep pace with the whirlwind of change driven by AI.

The rapid advancement of AI technology creates significant hurdles for those in charge of setting regulations. Typically, rules are created in response to established technologies or practices, but AI is anything but typical. It's a fast-changing field, marked by constant updates and advancements. Policymakers find themselves in a race to understand and regulate technologies that are still evolving. This challenge is made even tougher by the fact that AI overlaps with various fields like data science, ethics, law, and economics, creating a tangled web of issues that call for teamwork across different sectors.

To successfully navigate this complex terrain, it's vital for policymakers to team up with technologists, ethicists, and lawmakers to craft a regulatory framework that not only addresses the issues of today but also anticipates future challenges. This teamwork is essential for fully grasping how AI technologies affect society. Insights from technologists can shine a light on how algorithms work, which can inform ethical considerations. Meanwhile, lawmakers can offer a legal lens through which to balance innovation and public good. Without this collaborative approach, regulatory efforts might overlook crucial details and risks that could lead to unintended problems.

Looking at existing regulatory frameworks across different regions, it's clear there isn't a one-size-fits-all answer. The European Union, for instance, has made significant progress with its proposed AI Act, aiming to create a thorough regulatory landscape for AI technologies. This ambitious plan categorizes AI systems by their risk levels and sets strict requirements for high-risk applications. While the EU's proactive approach shows an awareness of AI's potential dangers, it also raises concerns that too many regulations could stifle innovation and growth. Finding the right balance between protecting people and encouraging technological progress is a delicate challenge.

On the other hand, the United States has taken a more fragmented approach to AI regulation. With different agencies overseeing various aspects of AI, the absence of a cohesive national strategy has resulted in a confusing patchwork of regulations for both developers and users. This disjointed system can create gaps in oversight, leaving some areas vulnerable to misuse or harmful practices. For example, the lack of strict rules around bias in AI algorithms has resulted in unfair outcomes in crucial sectors like hiring and law enforcement, highlighting the urgent need for a more unified and proactive regulatory approach.

International cooperation is another pressing challenge we can't ignore. Since AI development spans the globe, countries need to work together to create consistent standards that prevent a race to the bottom in terms of regulation. As nations compete to attract AI talent and investment, there's a risk that some may prioritize easing regulations over protecting public safety. This scenario emphasizes the need for international agreements that set minimum standards for AI governance, ensuring ethical considerations are upheld no matter where they occur.

Another significant issue in the regulatory landscape is the tendency for regulations to react to problems instead of proactively addressing them. History shows us that waiting for a crisis to hit before implementing rules often leads to inadequate responses that fail to tackle the root issues. For instance, the financial crisis of 2008 exposed serious weaknesses in the regulations governing banks and financial institutions. Similarly, if AI technologies are rolled out without proper oversight, we could face crises that might have been avoided with a more preemptive approach. Lawmakers must adopt a forward-looking mindset, predicting potential risks and creating regulations that don't just react but also prevent problems before they arise.

Public engagement and education play a crucial role in the regulatory process. Involving citizens in conversations about AI and its impacts helps build a more informed society, capable of contributing to the democratic process. Public discussions can shape regulatory approaches, making sure that policies reflect the values and concerns of the communities they impact. Moreover, educating the public about AI technologies demystifies the subject, empowering individuals to think critically about information and take part in the regulatory process.

One great example of public engagement is the growing push for "AI literacy" initiatives that aim to teach the general public about AI technologies, their capabilities, and their societal implications. By equipping citizens with knowledge about how AI works, we empower them to participate in discussions surrounding ethical usage, potential biases, and the need for regulation. This grassroots engagement can lead to a stronger democratic process, where individuals advocate for sensible regulations that prioritize the greater good.

Additionally, including diverse voices in the regulatory dialogue can bring to light different perspectives and experiences that might otherwise be missed. Marginalized communities, for example, often face the brunt of the unintended consequences that can arise from AI technologies, such as algorithmic bias. By involving these communities in the conversation about regulatory frameworks, policymakers can better understand their concerns and work towards creating inclusive regulations that protect everyone, not just a select few.

An inspiring example of this approach can be seen in the rise of community-led initiatives that advocate for responsible AI practices. These grassroots movements stress the importance of transparency and accountability, pushing for algorithms that can be audited and made accessible for public scrutiny. Such initiatives can encourage collaboration between technologists and activists, leading to a more equitable regulatory environment that prioritizes the well-being of society as a whole.

As we navigate the changing landscape of AI governance, it's crucial to recognize that adaptability in regulation is key. Given the rapid pace of technological change, regulatory frameworks should be designed to evolve alongside AI innovations. This can be accomplished by setting up processes for regular review and adjustment, ensuring that regulations stay relevant and effective over time. Policymakers should be open to learning from both successes and failures, using data-driven insights to refine regulations and address new challenges as they arise.

While the challenges of regulating AI technologies are significant, they also present a chance for a collaborative effort that spans different sectors and disciplines. This is an opportunity to build a system that not only protects public interests but also encourages innovation and ethical practices. By fostering collaboration among experts, engaging the public, and focusing on adaptability, we can create a regulatory environment that acknowledges the complexities of AI while serving the common good.

In this ever-changing landscape, we must not shy away from bold and innovative regulatory strategies. As we look ahead, we need to harness the potential of AI for positive change, ensuring these technologies are developed and used in ways that benefit society as a whole. The road ahead may be filled with challenges, but with a dedicated effort, we can carve out a path toward a more fair and just future in the age of artificial intelligence.

Ultimately, the need for effective regulation of AI technologies goes beyond mere compliance; it's about upholding democratic values and ensuring that the benefits of AI are shared fairly. As we work towards a future where technology enhances human well-being, the regulatory landscape must adapt to meet the challenges and opportunities that lie ahead. With collaboration, transparency, and public engagement leading the way, we can create a governance framework that upholds ethical principles and encourages innovation while protecting the rights of individuals and communities. In this age of rapid technological change, the stakes are high, and the time to act is now. The journey toward responsible AI governance is a shared one, calling for commitment and vision from everyone involved.

Chapter 6: Surveillance Capitalism and Social Control

Data as Capital

In a world where almost every part of our lives is becoming digital, the idea of treating data as capital is having a huge impact on our economy and society. The way personal data has turned into a commodity isn't just changing businesses; it's also changing how we relate to our own information. As we navigate this new landscape, it's crucial to grasp how our data has shifted from being a simple byproduct of our online activities to a valuable currency that corporations, governments, and other organizations use to gain profit and power.

Digital platforms like Facebook, Google, and Amazon have developed a strong craving for data. Every click, swipe, and interaction we have online is carefully tracked, analyzed, and repackaged. The massive amount of data generated each day isn't just a side effect of our online lives; it's the raw material that powers a new economic engine. In this new reality, data has transformed from just bits and bytes into a crucial asset that can be bought, sold, and traded.

To really understand this, let's look at just how much data we're creating. Estimates show that the world now produces around 2.5 quintillion bytes of data every single day. This incredible amount reflects the many sensors, mobile devices, and connected technologies that are all around us. This data is capital—valuable capital that tech giants use to create predictive models, targeted advertising, and personalized experiences that keep us engaged and spending.

So, what does this mean for everyday people? The way we treat personal data as a product raises important questions about our privacy, freedom, and sense of identity. When our data becomes a commodity, we risk being reduced to simple data points, losing our individuality and complexity. Our likes, habits, and even who we are can be simplified into algorithms that determine how different systems treat us. The effects of this are significant, reaching into our shopping habits and affecting the very fabric of our society and democratic processes.

Take targeted advertising, for example. Personalizing ads isn't just a nice touch; it's a well-planned strategy meant to influence our choices. This raises serious concerns about consent. Are people really aware of what they're agreeing to when they click "I agree" on those long terms and conditions? Often, the answer is no. The fine print in these agreements often hides the reality of how our data is collected and used, leaving many in the dark about how their information is being turned into a product.

The impact of a data-driven economy goes well beyond just shopping. Many sectors—such as healthcare, law enforcement, and education—are increasingly relying on data for decision-making, which raises critical issues about fairness and accountability. Algorithms that are trained on past data can continue existing inequalities, leading to outcomes that hurt marginalized groups. This begs the question: who is really benefiting from this data economy, and at what cost to others?

Additionally, as data becomes a major source of economic value, a few corporations hold a lot of power. The tech giants of today, who control enormous amounts of data, are often compared to the industrial leaders of the Gilded Age. They wield significant influence over our economy and society, and this concentration of power is concerning. It threatens competition and democratic governance. The risks of manipulation, surveillance, and control are real, as our data can be tracked, analyzed, and misused in ways we might not fully understand.

Given this, the role of government and regulatory bodies becomes very important. Policymakers are facing the tough job of creating rules that protect our privacy while also encouraging innovation and growth. Finding the right balance is tricky; strict regulations could hinder progress, while too little oversight could lead to abuses. There's an urgent need for strong data protection laws and ethical guidelines for collecting and using our data.

Raising public awareness and providing education are key in this environment. People need to feel empowered to understand the worth of their data and what it means when it's treated like a product. A digitally aware society can navigate the complex world of the digital economy with confidence and informed choices. By promoting a culture of understanding and advocacy, we can start to take back control over our personal information in a world where it often seems like it's just a commodity for corporations.

When we think about how data has transformed into capital, it's clear that the effects are deep and wide-ranging. The commercialization of personal data isn't just an economic shift; it's a societal change that challenges our values, privacy, and our identities. We need a collective response that supports ethical standards, accountability, and individual rights. Only by working together can we change how we view data and make sure it benefits society as a whole, rather than just a select few.

In this journey, our understanding of data as capital needs to include a keen look at the systems that govern it. Creating a fairer digital future takes vigilance, advocacy, and a commitment to redefining our engagement with surveillance capitalism. We, as individuals, have the power to demand transparency, accountability, and ethical conduct from those who want to use our data. It's a call to action that should resonate throughout society, pushing us to stand up for our rights in an age where data has become the new oil—and we are its unwitting producers.

AI-Enabled Surveillance

The rise of artificial intelligence is opening new doors in the world of surveillance, bringing both excitement and anxiety. As technology becomes a part of our everyday lives, AI tools for monitoring are getting smarter and are spreading through our public and private spaces at a rapid pace. Facial recognition systems, predictive analytics, and behavior tracking technologies aren't just cool gadgets; they are powerful forces changing our social norms, personal freedoms, and what privacy really means.

At the center of this shift is a range of surveillance tools. Take facial recognition technology, for example. It's an incredible advancement that can pick out people in a crowd with surprising accuracy. Cameras fitted with AI algorithms are popping up everywhere—from airports to busy city streets—scanning faces, gathering data, and building databases that can connect identities to actions, movements, and affiliations instantly. Imagine strolling down a crowded street, and without you even knowing, your face is captured, analyzed, and stored in a system accessible to law enforcement, businesses, or even shady entities.

Predictive analytics goes even further. This technology sifts through massive amounts of data to predict what people might do next. Think of it as a digital crystal ball that helps organizations anticipate everything from shopping trends to possible criminal behavior. For example, police departments can use these systems to figure out where crimes might happen based on past data. While the goal may be to keep the public safe, it raises serious questions about fairness, accuracy, and bias. The more we depend on these predictive tools, the higher the chances of reinforcing existing inequalities in society.

Behavior tracking technologies add another layer to our increasingly scrutinized lives. From the apps on our phones to smart home gadgets, every move we make with technology is being logged, analyzed, and often turned into profit. Social media platforms, for instance, use complex algorithms that don't just track what we like and share; they also shape the information we see, influencing our perspectives and social interactions. This creates a feedback loop where our behavior is constantly assessed and modified, leading to a skewed sense of freedom that deserves our attention.

Urban surveillance systems are a clear example of this trend, as cities install AI cameras to keep an eye on public areas under the pretense of safety. Supporters argue these systems can lower crime rates and speed up emergency responses, but critics point out the chilling effect they have on personal freedoms. People start to feel like they're always being watched, which leads to something known as the "Panopticon Effect." This term comes from philosopher Jeremy Bentham's idea of a prison design where inmates, knowing they could be observed at any time, regulate their own behavior. The consequences of this surveillance culture go beyond simple observation; they change how we interact with each other and our environment.

Think about the workplace, where monitoring software keeps an eye on employee productivity through keystroke tracking and screen recording. While businesses might say these measures help ensure productivity and accountability, they also foster a sense of distrust and stress. Workers may feel pressured to change their behavior to meet perceived expectations, which can stifle creativity and innovation. There's a tricky balance between improving workplace efficiency and respecting personal freedom that currently leans too much toward constant monitoring, raising important ethical questions.

The impacts of AI-driven surveillance stretch far and wide. As these technologies become more common, our privacy has diminished, leading to a culture where people feel compelled to conform and censor themselves. Many alter their actions out of fear of being monitored, creating a society where going along with the crowd is the norm and dissent gets silenced. This has serious implications for civil liberties; when people feel like they're under constant watch, their freedom to speak out and their right to privacy are put at risk.

As we think about these broader issues, the potential for misuse by both government and private businesses becomes crystal clear. In a world where data holds power, there's a constant temptation to abuse surveillance tools. Governments might use these technologies to stifle dissent or target marginalized groups, while companies could exploit personal data to manipulate consumer behavior without caring about ethics. The systems meant to protect individual rights need to adapt as technology advances, ensuring that ethical guidelines are in place when using surveillance tools.

However, not all stories about AI-enabled surveillance are negative. In some cases, these technologies can have a positive impact. For example, facial recognition can help locate missing persons or victims of trafficking, and predictive analytics can improve how resources are allocated in emergency situations. Yet, these advantages must be balanced with the ethical concerns they bring. The challenge is to find a way to make the most of AI's capabilities to benefit society while still respecting fundamental rights.

To illustrate this, think about urban policing in cities that have implemented AI surveillance systems. On one hand, places like Los Angeles have reported drops in crime rates, attributing this success to the effectiveness of surveillance technologies. But this success comes with a price. There have been instances of racial profiling and discriminatory practices associated with these systems, sparking public outrage and calls for accountability. Critics argue that the data used to train these algorithms often reflects historical biases, creating a cycle of inequality that disproportionately affects communities of color.

These real-life examples highlight how crucial it is to consider ethics when deploying surveillance technologies. Policymakers, tech developers, and society as a whole need to engage in meaningful conversations about the impacts of these tools. Pushing for stronger regulations and oversight is vital to prevent misuse and protect individual rights. It's not enough to just create new technologies; we also need to prioritize ethical standards that align with our societal values.

Education is key in this conversation. A society that understands technology is better prepared to tackle the challenges of AI-enabled surveillance. By raising awareness about what these technologies mean, individuals can better understand their rights and push for transparency in how their data is used. Knowing how surveillance works gives citizens the power to question and challenge practices that could infringe on their freedoms.

In today's world of surveillance capitalism, we all share the responsibility of redefining our relationship with technology. As AI evolves, so must our understanding of its effects on personal freedom, social control, and ethical governance. The connection between technology and society requires vigilance, advocacy, and a commitment to ensuring these powerful tools serve the common good rather than deepen systemic inequalities.

In the end, we must find a balanced way to embrace the potential upsides of AI-enabled surveillance while staunchly protecting our civil liberties. Each of us needs to stay engaged and informed, advocating for transparency, fairness, and ethical standards in how these technologies are used. The story of AI surveillance is still unfolding, and it's up to us to steer its direction, making sure our rights are upheld in a world increasingly shaped by algorithms and surveillance systems. Our future isn't set in stone; it's shaped by the choices and actions we take today.

The Changing Landscape of Privacy

We live in a time where privacy is both recognized as important and often given up without a second thought. With the rise of technology and constant connectivity, privacy isn't just seen as a basic right anymore; it feels more like something we can trade away for ease, social connection, or the perks that tech offers. Each new app, gadget, or service tempts us with the promise of a smoother experience, sometimes at the expense of our own privacy.

Gone are the simple days when a chat could happen without anyone eavesdropping or when we could send a letter without worrying about who might peek at it along the way. Now, every click, tap, and swipe leaves a mark on our digital lives. We exist in a world where the "like" buttons on social media earn money for companies, and our online habits are analyzed to create detailed profiles that influence everything from the ads we see to how we think about politics. We've become so used to being watched—by both the government and private companies—that we hardly notice these invasions of privacy anymore.

Many people find themselves in a tough spot: they want the latest technology or social media platform that promises to make life better, but they know they're giving up bits of their privacy to get it. Take smartphones, for instance—these devices are everywhere, acting as both our communication lifelines and little surveillance tools that track our locations, habits, and interactions. Each time there's an update or a new feature, users are bombarded with privacy policies that seem to grow more complicated and confusing. Many just scroll through the terms and conditions as if they're a boring formality, rather than something that could greatly affect their lives.

As we get used to this trade-off, the effects ripple out from our personal lives into society as a whole. Trust, which used to be a key part of relationships, starts to fade. People become cautious about who can see their information and how it might be used against them. This uncertainty seeps into friendships and family connections, making people hold back, worried that their thoughts and actions could be monitored or twisted. This can lead to self-censorship, where individuals adjust their behavior to fit what they think is acceptable to others.

The cultural shifts brought on by these changing privacy norms also raise important questions about personal freedom. When people give up their privacy for the sake of convenience, they can end up stuck in a cycle of following the crowd. Social media encourages everyone to share every moment of their lives, pushing us into a culture where true authenticity is judged by the number of likes and followers we have. This constant chase for validation can wear down self-esteem, leading people to focus more on getting approval than on building real relationships.

The consequences of losing privacy go beyond personal connections; they change the way society itself communicates. When surveillance becomes the norm, dissenting voices can feel silenced. If people think they're under a microscope, they might hold back from sharing opinions that go against the grain. This chilling effect can be especially harmful in democracies, where the ability to voice differing viewpoints is crucial for healthy discussions and progress.

Marginalized communities often feel the harshest effects of invasive surveillance. When monitoring becomes commonplace, it can worsen existing inequalities, as these groups may find themselves unfairly targeted by both government and corporate watchfulness. The problems escalate when these communities cannot fight for their rights, leading to deeper roots of injustice in society.

As we navigate this shifting landscape of privacy, it's crucial to realize that we're not just passively accepting new technologies. Our changing relationship with privacy reflects larger cultural and psychological shifts—an ever-changing mix influenced by technology, personal choices, and societal norms. The values we cherish as a community will shape how we approach these changes and the choices we make about balancing privacy and convenience.

To tackle the challenges this new environment brings, it's important for individuals to rethink how they view privacy. Learning and awareness are key. By understanding the impact of their choices, people can start to engage more critically with technology and ask for clearer answers from the companies and governments that gather their information. This change in mindset can help reclaim a sense of control over personal data and encourage a culture that values privacy as a basic right instead of something to negotiate away.

The evolving landscape of privacy points to a bigger trend in society—a move towards being more connected, yet oddly isolated at the same time. As we work through these complexities, understanding the importance of privacy in our lives is vital. It's up to each of us to advocate for a future where our individual rights aren't traded off for progress, where conversations about privacy are revitalized, and where trust once again becomes a cornerstone of how we interact with each other and the technologies that fill our lives.

In this fast-changing world, we need to ask ourselves: how do we set our boundaries as individuals and as a society to ensure we don't lose sight of the value of privacy while enjoying the conveniences technology brings? As we think through these important questions, it's clear that the decisions we make today will shape our tomorrow—a future where the value of privacy is something we protect fiercely and view not just as a personal right, but as a crucial part of our society.

Chapter 7: Social Stratification and Mobility

Erosion of the Middle Class

The middle class has long been seen as the heart of our society, a crucial support system that holds up economic stability and community spirit. Traditionally, this group has been linked to upward mobility, home ownership, and the steady income that helps families plan for their futures. Yet, in recent years, we've started to notice a worrying trend: the slow decline of the middle class, and the rise of artificial intelligence is significantly influencing this change. Job losses, stagnant wages, and increasing living costs are all playing a part in this decline. By taking a closer look at these trends, we can better understand what they mean for our society as a whole.

To really get a sense of the impact of this decline, we should first recognize the historical importance of the middle class. It hasn't just been an economic power; it has also been a stabilizing force in society. A strong middle class fosters community ties and responsibility, encouraging people to engage with civic duties and political activities. When the middle class starts to shrink, it leaves a gap that can upset the balance of society, leading to greater inequality and unrest.

Today's economic landscape isn't just shaped by traditional financial forces; it's also deeply connected to advances in technology, especially artificial intelligence and automation. These changes have dramatically altered the job market, creating a divide where high-skill, well-paying jobs flourish while low-skill, low-paying jobs abound. This split has made it harder for those in the middle to find good opportunities, leaving many struggling to find stable, well-paying work.

Consider the manufacturing sector, which was once a hallmark of the American middle class. The rise of automation has drastically changed this industry. Factories that used to hire thousands now rely on robots for production, leading to the disappearance of many jobs. While there's still demand for skilled labor, the entry points for workers without specialized training have become very narrow. As a result, former factory employees are left to navigate a job market that offers limited options or low-paying jobs with no chance for growth.

Retail has faced a similar challenge. The boom of online shopping has transformed the retail landscape, resulting in the closure of countless physical stores. Many people who once worked as cashiers, sales associates, and stockroom managers now have to either find new jobs in a shrinking industry or look for low-wage work in other sectors. Even as new opportunities arise in tech-driven retail, many of these positions require skills that displaced workers may not have, further widening the economic gap.

The service industry, which once provided a variety of middle-class jobs, now feels unstable and uncertain. The rapid growth of gig economy platforms has changed the way many people approach work, often leading to jobs that lack benefits and security. Workers in this space often find themselves caught in a cycle of part-time gigs, struggling to pay the bills while lacking any real path for advancement. The promise of flexible work often hides the grim reality of economic hardship.

As we think about these changing dynamics, we must also tackle the economic factors that have worsened the decline of the middle class. Wage stagnation has become a long-lasting problem, with many workers seeing little to no pay increase over the past few decades. Meanwhile, the cost of living keeps climbing due to rising housing prices, healthcare costs, and education fees. The combination of stagnant wages and rising expenses creates a tough situation for middle-class families, making it harder for them to maintain their way of life.

In this divided economy, the social fabric begins to tear. With fewer chances for upward mobility, frustration grows, and community bonds weaken. The middle class is no longer the engine of economic growth; instead, it serves as a reminder of what used to be. The gap between rich and poor widens, as access to resources becomes a privilege for the few, leaving many feeling alienated and powerless.

To truly understand the implications of today's middle class struggles, we can look back at the Gilded Age, a time marked by stark economic inequality and social turmoil. During that period, technological advancements led to immense wealth for some, while others lived in poverty. The concentration of wealth among a small elite caused a sharp divide, sparking social unrest and demands for change. Just like the Gilded Age highlighted the dangers of unchecked capitalism and tech disruption, today's situation is showing us similar patterns.

The similarities are striking. In both cases, rapid technological advancements have reshaped job markets, leaving many people struggling to adapt. The wealthy reap the rewards while the middle class faces challenges that threaten their very survival. The lessons from history are clear: without meaningful action, we risk repeating the mistakes that led to the inequalities of the Gilded Age.

As we face the decline of the middle class, the role of policy becomes incredibly important. Lawmakers have a pressing responsibility to revitalize this vital group, ensuring that the benefits of technological changes aren't enjoyed by just a select few. Investing in education and training is crucial to help workers gain the skills needed for the jobs of the future. Creating accessible opportunities for reskilling and upskilling can help individuals move from declining industries to those that are growing.

Fair economic policies must also be a priority. This includes addressing wage stagnation by raising the minimum wage and implementing practices that promote fair labor conditions. Additionally, affordable housing initiatives and healthcare reforms can ease the financial burdens faced by middle-class families. By enacting policies that encourage economic inclusivity, we can begin to mend the fraying fabric of society and foster a sense of shared responsibility.

The responsibility doesn't rest solely on policymakers. Businesses also play a crucial role in shaping the future of the middle class. Companies should prioritize fair practices that consider the well-being of their workers, understanding that a healthy middle class is good for their business too. By investing in their employees and promoting a culture of growth and development, companies can help create a vibrant economy that works for everyone.

Looking to the future, it's crucial to recognize the urgent need to address the decline of the middle class. The lessons from our past remind us that without decisive action, we risk entering a new era of inequality reminiscent of the Gilded Age. By prioritizing policies that support the middle class and investing in our workforce, we can build a society that values inclusivity, opportunity, and shared success.

The erosion of the middle class isn't just an economic issue; it's a social crisis that demands our attention and action. The challenges we face are complex and multifaceted, but they are not impossible to overcome. By coming together to advocate for fair practices and policies, we can work toward a future where the middle class thrives once more, serving as a bedrock of stability in society. The stakes are high, and the time to act is now.

Barriers to Upward Mobility

In a time when artificial intelligence is set to change our economy, the idea of moving up in the world isn't just about personal dreams or hard work. It's a deeper look at the systemic barriers that exist in our society. These obstacles are woven into our economic and educational systems, making it difficult for many people to access the opportunities they need. Not everyone has the same access to quality education, professional connections, and technology, and these differences only highlight the hurdles faced by those trying to improve their lives. To really understand how these barriers interact with new technologies, we need to take a closer look at them.

Let's start by discussing educational inequalities. The groundwork for moving up often begins in the classroom. The reality is clear: the education a child receives can be heavily influenced by where they live, their family's income, and the resources available— or sadly, the ones that are missing—at their school. In the U.S., public schools are mostly funded by local property taxes, which creates a significant imbalance. Wealthier communities can invest more in their schools, while those in poorer areas struggle with overcrowded classrooms, outdated supplies, and a lack of extracurricular activities that help develop important skills.

Imagine a child in a well-funded school district. They have access to advanced courses, cutting-edge technology, and programs that teach teamwork and leadership. On the flip side, a child in a less fortunate district may find themselves in crowded classrooms with too few teachers, old computers, and a curriculum that fails to engage them. The gap between these experiences isn't just about the quality of education; it shapes their future opportunities or shuts them down altogether.

Recently, the rise of artificial intelligence has brought both exciting possibilities and challenges to education. Personalized learning tools powered by AI can create tailored learning experiences for each student, which is fantastic for those who can access such technologies. However, for millions who stay on the wrong side of the digital divide, this promise feels like a distant dream. The inequalities in classroom technology reflect the larger social inequities we see everywhere. While some students benefit from advanced resources, many others lack the basic tools necessary to reach their potential.

The effects of educational inequalities extend far beyond graduation. Access to quality education is closely tied to economic opportunities later in life. Those who don't receive proper preparation often end up in lower-paying jobs, trapping them—and sometimes their families—in a cycle of poverty that can last for generations. This cycle is heartbreaking: families struggling financially often can't invest in their children's education, making it even harder for the next generation to break free. In this way, the educational system can serve as a ladder to success for some while acting as a barrier for others.

Now, let's look at the economic barriers that also hold back upward mobility. Many view higher education as a key step toward achieving their dreams, but for many, the cost of tuition can be overwhelming. The student debt crisis is alarming, with graduates facing loans that feel impossible to repay. This financial burden hits marginalized communities especially hard, where getting loans can be a real struggle. The irony is clear: the very route to success that education promises can turn into a trap, locking graduates into financial struggles for years.

Additionally, as living costs rise, people are forced to decide whether to invest in their education or focus on immediate financial needs. With soaring prices for housing, healthcare, and basic necessities, many individuals find it tough to prioritize college. In this situation, pursuing a degree becomes a luxury that many simply cannot afford. When the path to upward mobility is tied to expensive education, those without the means to pay are left behind, widening the gap between those who have and those who struggle.

Entrepreneurship, often seen as a route to economic independence, is also full of hurdles. For those looking to start their own businesses, finding funding can be especially tough. Traditional lenders typically prefer established businesses or entrepreneurs with solid credit—criteria that are often out of reach for those from economically disadvantaged backgrounds. This exclusion from financial networks that offer startup capital stifles innovation and opportunity for underrepresented communities, reinforcing a cycle of poverty that's hard to break.

The mix of educational and economic barriers paints a bleak picture for those hoping to move up in life. These obstacles are made worse by a job market that is constantly changing due to technology. As AI disrupts traditional jobs, the demand for skilled labor increases while low-skill jobs decrease. Those without access to quality education or the means to learn new skills are left behind. This creates a workforce that is not only divided by income but also by skills and opportunities.

Yet, amid these challenges, we should recognize the vital role that social networks and mentorship play in upward mobility. The connections people make often become essential for career growth and new opportunities. For those from wealthier families, networking comes easily. They have access to professionals who can help with guidance, internships, and job placements. This network can give them a boost into desirable careers, reinforcing a cycle of privilege and opportunity.

In sharp contrast, individuals from lower-income backgrounds often lack these connections. They may try to navigate the job market without the support that comes from a strong professional network. The absence of mentorship can be a huge hurdle since many job openings are filled through referrals rather than job listings. This exclusion from vital networking opportunities traps people in poverty and limits their chances for advancement.

Fortunately, there are inspiring stories of resilience that highlight how some individuals have successfully navigated these barriers. Take, for example, a young woman from a low-income area who, despite facing educational disadvantages and limited mentorship, actively sought resources to better her situation. She made use of online platforms that offered free courses, developing her skills in technology and data analysis. Through hard work and determination, she secured an internship at a prestigious tech firm.

Her journey shows the grit needed to overcome systemic challenges. She utilized every available resource, creating a supportive network of peers and mentors along the way. By engaging with local programs aimed at connecting underrepresented individuals with industry professionals, she opened up new opportunities for herself. Her story isn't an isolated case; it reflects the experiences of many people who refuse to let their circumstances define them. Instead, they find ways to succeed, using their unique perspectives and creativity to carve out a space in a world that often seems tilted against them.

These stories of victory remind us of the resilience of the human spirit and underscore the importance of creating pathways for upward mobility. They highlight the urgent need for systemic changes to remove the barriers that hold so many people back. By investing in better educational access, affordable college options, and mentorship programs, society can work toward leveling the playing field and ensuring that moving up is a possibility for everyone, not just a select few.

The barriers to upward mobility are complex and deeply rooted in the structures that determine who gets access to opportunities. Education, economic resources, and social networks are all vital aspects that can either help lift individuals up or keep them stuck in cycles of poverty. As we navigate the challenges of an economy influenced by AI, it's crucial that we tackle these systemic barriers head-on. Only through dedicated efforts at community, corporate, and governmental levels can we build a society that values inclusivity and fair chances for all.

As we reflect on the implications of our tech-driven world, we should let the lessons learned from those who have made it through these hurdles guide us. Building a future where everyone has a shot at success calls for a commitment to breaking down barriers and creating an environment where resilience can thrive. This responsibility doesn't just fall on individuals striving to rise above their situations; it's a shared obligation for society— to ensure that everyone, no matter their starting point, has the chance to reach their full potential. The journey toward upward mobility thus becomes a collective mission to uplift entire communities, paving the way for a brighter, more equitable future for everyone.

Cultural and Social Divides

As we find ourselves stepping into a new era shaped by artificial intelligence, we can't help but notice the growing cultural and social divides around us. The rise of AI isn't just a story about technological progress; it's a complex situation that unfolds against a backdrop of economic inequality, which is widening the gaps between different groups in our society. This divide goes beyond just wealth; it digs deeper, creating feelings of alienation and disenfranchisement that weaken the very foundation of our communities. The tensions that arise from this inequality create an environment where divisions are not just noticed but are made worse by the very tools meant to uplift us.

The psychological effects of economic inequality are significant, impacting the lives of those who feel left behind as AI changes the landscape. Picture waking up each day in a world where your opportunities depend not on your hard work or skills, but on an algorithm that mainly serves a privileged few. This sense of being left out is deeply felt. It builds a mentality of "us versus them," where those who have access to the latest technologies see themselves as separate from those struggling with feelings of obsolescence and exclusion. This polarization isn't just a side effect of technological advancement; it points to a deeper societal issue that, if ignored, could tear apart the threads of community and togetherness.

As individuals struggle with their place in a society that increasingly rewards a select few, their psychological well-being begins to unravel. Frustration, hopelessness, and resentment can grow, leading to a widespread feeling of isolation. This sense of being disconnected often shows itself in various ways, like increased mental health challenges or a rise in substance abuse, as people try to cope with their feelings of disenfranchisement. At its core, the psychological toll of economic inequality pushes people away from the supportive bonds of community they once relied on. As the social fabric frays, a dangerous polarization takes root, creating a divide that's tough to bridge.

While we navigate this challenging landscape, it's crucial to recognize that the weakening of community ties often goes hand-in-hand with these divides. The traditional connections that once held neighborhoods together become strained as economic differences push people into focusing on their own interests. The days when neighbors would support and stand by each other seem to be fading, leaving us in a world filled with strangers who share space but lack connection. The fallout from this erosion goes far beyond social interactions; it directly affects political involvement and civic responsibility. A disconnected community is more vulnerable to the seductive simplicity of populist messages, which often thrive in environments marked by perceived injustice and disenfranchisement.

Populism can be seen as a response to the frustration of those who feel their voices are drowned out by the privileged few. In a time when the advantages of AI and automation seem to benefit only a small group, the cries from the masses grow louder. Political movements that seize upon this unrest often frame their messages in terms of blame, targeting "the elite" while promising to return power to "the people." However, this approach comes with its own set of challenges, as simple solutions rarely tackle the complex issues involved. In fact, they might deepen existing divides, fostering an "us versus them" mindset that further alienates people from each other and from the political process.

The decline of civic responsibility is another troubling trend. When community connections weaken, individuals often retreat into their own lives, focusing on personal survival rather than the well-being of the group. Civic engagement suffers as people become less motivated to participate in local governance or community efforts that could build unity. This lack of involvement leads to a cycle that keeps inequality in place, as communities lacking active engagement become easy targets for exploitative practices. The very systems designed to help can turn into instruments of oppression when people fail to come together and hold them accountable.

Yet, amid the challenges posed by these divides, there's a spark of hope. There are ways to heal these rifts, and it's vital if we want to build a more inclusive society. Community engagement, open dialogue, and collaboration need to become the pillars of our efforts to close the gaps that separate us. We should actively seek out and uplift the voices of those who have often been pushed aside, creating safe spaces where their stories can be heard and appreciated. Only through honest conversations can we start to break down the stereotypes and misunderstandings that drive us apart.

We can look to successful initiatives that promote understanding and inclusion, as they offer blueprints for how we can move forward together. Community-led programs that focus on sharing skills, mentorship, and collaborative approaches to local problems can become powerful tools for rebuilding connections. These initiatives do more than tackle economic disparities; they nurture a sense of belonging and shared purpose that can breathe new life into communities. By focusing on collaboration instead of competition, we can create environments where individuals feel empowered to work for the greater good rather than isolating themselves.

Education also plays a crucial role in bridging these divides. By ensuring that everyone has access to quality education, we can cultivate a sense of shared destiny among individuals from all backgrounds. When we invest in programs that provide resources, mentorship, and networking for underrepresented groups, we don't just empower individuals; we enrich our communities as a whole. Education is a great equalizer, and when we treat it as a shared value, we can start to break down the barriers that keep people apart.

We can't ignore the impact of technology in this conversation either. While artificial intelligence and automation have contributed to societal gaps, they also have the potential to be tools for positive change. By purposefully designing AI systems that prioritize inclusivity and accessibility, we can create technologies that bring people together instead of pushing them apart. Imagine platforms that promote community engagement, enhance collaboration, and amplify the voices of those who are often overlooked. Such innovations could help level the playing field, allowing everyone to benefit from the positive aspects of technology.

Ultimately, the way forward lies in recognizing our shared humanity. The divides we see aren't impossible to overcome; they reflect the choices we make as a society. By cultivating empathy, understanding, and a commitment to progress as a group, we can start to bridge the gaps that separate us. This journey will take time and effort, but the benefits are immense. A society built on inclusivity, understanding, and cooperation is one where everyone has the chance to thrive, free from the chains of inequality.

We don't have to look very far to find examples of communities that have successfully faced these divides. Initiatives focused on dialogue, creativity, and engagement have transformed fractured neighborhoods into thriving hubs of support and collaboration. These stories inspire us and remind us that change is achievable; they also serve as a call to action for all of us. Each of us has a role to play in this effort, whether through volunteering, advocating for change, or simply being a good neighbor.

As we consider the effects of cultural and social divides made worse by AI, it's clear that addressing these issues isn't just the job of policymakers or tech companies. It's a shared responsibility that invites each of us to take action in our own circles. By promoting inclusivity and understanding, we can ignite conversations that bridge these divides and pave the way for a future where the benefits of technology are enjoyed by everyone.

In this fast-changing world, the choice is in our hands. We can either accept the divisions that threaten to pull us apart or work together to build a society that reflects our shared values of fairness, connection, and hope. The road to healing these cultural and social divides may be tough, but it's a journey worth taking—a journey that can lead to a fairer and more equitable world for generations to come.

Chapter 8: Ethical Dilemmas and AI Bias

Bias in AI Systems: An Unjust Reflection of Society

The world around us is a rich and colorful mix of different cultures, experiences, and viewpoints. However, it's a bit ironic that the technology aimed at improving our lives often reflects the biases and inequalities already present in society. This is especially true when it comes to artificial intelligence (AI). The algorithms designed by people can sometimes mirror our prejudices. When we discuss bias in AI systems, we're not just talking about technical glitches; we're diving into a serious issue that questions our sense of fairness, equality, and what it means to be human together.

At the heart of artificial intelligence is data, but data isn't always a fair or accurate representation of reality. It's shaped by human experiences, which can be flawed and influenced by biases in our society. So, when AI systems are trained on historical data, they can unintentionally pick up and spread these existing inequalities. For instance, think about a hiring algorithm trained on resumes submitted to a tech company over the last ten years. If that company has mostly hired men in the past, the algorithm might favor resumes similar to those of previous candidates, inadvertently leaving out women and people from underrepresented backgrounds. This isn't just a technical mishap; it's a reinforcement of deep-rooted inequities in our society.

A striking example of this issue is facial recognition technology, which has been found to have serious racial biases. Research shows that these systems often misidentify people with darker skin tones much more frequently compared to their lighter-skinned counterparts. For instance, a 2018 study by the MIT Media Lab revealed that facial recognition software from leading tech companies misidentified the gender of dark-skinned women with an error rate over 30%, while the error rate for lighter-skinned men was less than 1%. This isn't just a minor oversight; it can lead to wrongful accusations, unfair profiling, and a breakdown of trust in law enforcement. As we move further into a digital age, these biases can continue to fuel systemic injustices that have existed for generations.

AI systems are used in sensitive areas like healthcare, finance, and law enforcement, where biased algorithms can change lives. Imagine an AI system deciding who qualifies for medical treatments. If that algorithm relies on historical data reflecting past healthcare inequalities—like the neglect of marginalized communities—it may deny crucial treatments to those who need them the most. This isn't just a hypothetical situation; studies have shown that such biases can lead to significant differences in patient care based on race and socioeconomic status. The sad truth is that the very technology meant to enhance our well-being can instead deepen the divides among us.

Another important factor in AI bias is its link to socioeconomic status. Algorithms often use data that includes income levels and education, which are influenced by societal structures that disadvantage certain groups. For example, think about a predictive policing algorithm that looks at crime data to decide where police should focus their efforts. If the data comes from neighborhoods that have been over-policed in the past, the algorithm may unfairly target these areas, creating a cycle of criminalization that further marginalizes the residents. This creates a self-fulfilling prophecy where past biases guide future policing strategies, perpetuating a cycle of inequality and distrust.

Fixing bias in AI systems is more than just a technical challenge; it's a responsibility we all share as a society. The stakes are high, and the effects reach far beyond technology into the fabric of our communities. To tackle these biases, we need to start by closely examining the data we rely on. This means committing to inclusive data collection practices that genuinely reflect the voices and experiences of marginalized groups. By ensuring our data sets capture the full diversity of society, we can help reduce the risk of reinforcing systemic inequalities with our algorithms.

Transparency and accountability in how AI is used must also be top priorities. Everyone involved—from tech companies to policymakers—needs to understand their role in creating these systems and the impacts they have. This includes rigorously testing algorithms for bias and providing channels for marginalized communities to share their concerns and experiences. Building diverse teams of developers, data scientists, and ethicists can bring a range of perspectives to the table, which helps foster more equitable outcomes.

As we face these ethical challenges, it's vital to spark a public conversation about AI bias. Awareness alone isn't enough; real change demands collective action. Advocating for clearer regulations can empower individuals and communities to hold tech companies accountable for their actions. By pushing for transparency and ethical practices in AI, we can begin to break down the structures that allow biases to thrive.

The connection between AI and societal bias is a crucial issue in our tech-driven world. It highlights not just the limitations of our algorithms but also the urgent need to rethink the values that guide our technological progress. As artificial intelligence continues to grow in importance in our lives, we must tackle these biases directly, making sure the systems we create do not just reflect past injustices but instead help us move toward a fairer future.

As we navigate the complicated landscape of AI bias, we also face the pressing question of accountability. When an algorithm makes a biased decision, who is to blame? Is it the programmer who wrote the code? The company that launched the algorithm? The society that allowed these biases to persist? Figuring out accountability in the age of AI requires a major shift in how we view technology and those who create it. We need to recognize that AI, being a product of human design, is intertwined with the ethical standards that guide our actions. This demands a strong effort to establish regulations that hold developers and companies responsible for the consequences of their algorithms.

In this light, the call for ethical AI isn't just a trend; it's a pressing necessity. Organizations are starting to understand that ethical considerations can no longer be an afterthought. They need to be a fundamental part of the development process from the very beginning. This involves creating diverse teams that can critically evaluate the potential impacts of their work and setting up a continuous feedback loop that invites input from affected communities. By making ethics a core component of AI development, we can build an environment that prioritizes fairness, justice, and inclusivity.

As we think about the future of AI, a crucial question remains: how can we ensure that these technologies uplift society instead of reinforcing existing inequalities? The answer lies in our dedication to being vigilant and taking action. This means actively confronting biases, advocating for transparency, and promoting accountability. It also calls for a strong belief in the possibility of a more equitable future—one where technology empowers us rather than oppresses us.

In the end, the path to tackling bias in AI systems isn't a job for just one person; it's a shared responsibility that requires collaboration across different fields and communities. It calls for the involvement of technologists, policymakers, ethicists, and everyday people. Together, we can create a framework that not only addresses the flaws in AI but also drives broader societal change. As we work to correct these injustices, we not only shape the future of technology but also redefine what it means to be human together. The challenge ahead is significant, but it's one we can overcome. We have the power to demand a future where artificial intelligence showcases the best in us rather than the worst.

Accountability and Transparency: Who's Responsible?

In today's fast-changing world of artificial intelligence, accountability and transparency are becoming key elements in creating an ethical foundation for this groundbreaking technology. As AI systems weave their way into our everyday lives, we must address important questions about responsibility—especially when these systems fail or lead to biased results. The answers to these questions aren't just theoretical; they have significant effects on individuals, communities, and society at large. A thoughtful approach to accountability and transparency can help steer us clear of the dangers of inaction and toward a future where AI benefits everyone, not just a privileged few.

One standout example of a regulatory framework aimed at boosting accountability in data processing is the General Data Protection Regulation (GDPR), which is in place across the European Union. The GDPR ensures that people have control over their personal data and highlights the need for organizations to be transparent about how they collect and use that data. It requires that users understand the reasoning behind automated decisions that impact them, promoting what is often called "explainable AI." This idea emphasizes the need for AI systems to be clear and understandable to regular users. Without this clarity, we risk growing distrust and facing harmful outcomes.

Consider a financial institution that uses AI to evaluate loan applications. If someone is denied a loan based on an algorithm that isn't properly explained, they may feel lost and confused. They might not know if the decision was based on their credit score, income, or something else entirely. This uncertainty can lead to frustration, diminish trust in the financial system, and deter individuals from seeking financial help in the future. Moreover, if there's no clear explanation, individuals can't effectively challenge decisions made by such systems, leaving them vulnerable to biased or discriminatory algorithms.

The importance of transparency becomes even clearer when looking at real-world examples where lack of accountability led to negative outcomes. A striking case involves hiring algorithms. A study found that a widely used recruitment tool was unintentionally biased against women. The algorithm was trained on resumes submitted over the past decade, which mostly came from male applicants. Consequently, the AI favored male candidates, worsening the existing gender gap in the tech field. Such examples highlight the real impact AI decisions can have on people's lives and raise crucial questions about who is accountable.

When AI systems are created without proper oversight, the risk of reinforcing systemic inequalities grows. This emphasizes the urgent need for strong regulatory frameworks that not only promote transparency but also ensure companies are held accountable for the effects of their algorithms. While many organizations have started to adopt ethical guidelines, the absence of enforceable regulations can lead to inconsistency in how those guidelines are followed. Responsibility for oversight can't rest solely on developers and companies; it needs to be a shared duty that includes policymakers, consumers, and civil society.

Engaging the public is vital for promoting accountability in the tech industry. Grassroots movements advocating for ethical technology have gained traction in recent years, showing how collective action can bring about real change. For instance, groups focused on digital rights have pushed for laws that require companies to be transparent and give individuals a voice in how their data is used. These efforts remind us that the public can influence policy and corporate behavior, advocating for a future where technology is developed with ethics at the forefront.

A powerful example of public involvement can be seen in the campaign against facial recognition technology. Activists and concerned individuals have raised concerns about the widespread use of this technology by law enforcement, which often carries biases and inaccuracies. Movements in various cities worldwide have led to temporary halts or outright bans on facial recognition by police forces. This collective action highlights the strength of civic engagement in shaping policy and holding tech companies accountable for the societal impacts of their products.

When we think about accountability and transparency, "explainable AI" is both a challenge and an opportunity. On one side, the technical intricacies of machine learning and AI can make transparency difficult. Algorithms often function as "black boxes," delivering results without revealing how they reached those conclusions. On the flip side, the push for explainable AI opens doors for innovation and advancements in the field. Developers and researchers are actively seeking ways to create AI systems that are easier to understand, ensuring that users grasp the reasons behind algorithmic decisions.

Take the healthcare industry, for example, where AI is increasingly used for diagnosing conditions and suggesting treatments. The stakes are incredibly high—imagine a patient getting a treatment recommendation from an algorithm that lacks transparency. If healthcare providers can't explain how the AI came to its conclusion, they risk losing their patients' trust and may even compromise patient safety. By aiming for transparency in AI applications within healthcare, we can ensure that patients are informed participants in their own care, allowing them to feel more in control of their health decisions.

The call for accountability becomes even more critical in areas where AI decisions can drastically change lives. In the criminal justice system, predictive policing algorithms have faced scrutiny for potentially reinforcing racial biases. If an algorithm suggests higher police presence in specific neighborhoods based on historical crime data, it may lead to over-policing in communities already grappling with systemic injustices. Therefore, it's essential for developers, law enforcement, and policymakers to be held accountable for addressing these issues. By enhancing transparency and encouraging public engagement, communities can demand accountability for the consequences of these technologies.

To cultivate a culture of accountability and transparency, it's essential to include a variety of perspectives in developing and deploying AI systems. Diverse teams can lead to deeper insights into how technology might impact different communities. It's crucial to prioritize the inclusion of voices from marginalized groups so their experiences and concerns are considered during the design process. By promoting an environment of collaboration and inclusivity, we can strive toward a technological landscape that values equity and justice.

Another vital aspect of ensuring transparency is establishing metrics to assess the performance of AI systems. Developers can conduct regular audits to evaluate algorithms for bias and effectiveness, ensuring these technologies align with ethical standards. Sharing the results of these audits publicly can further build trust and accountability, allowing consumers to make informed choices about the technology they engage with. Rather than seeing transparency as a burden, we should view it as an opportunity to showcase our dedication to ethical practices.

As we navigate the complexities of accountability and transparency in AI, we must also face the broader question of who is responsible when these systems fail. The answer is not straightforward and calls for a shift in how we think about technology and ethics. Blaming developers or companies alone isn't enough; we also need to reflect on the roles of policymakers, regulatory bodies, and society as a whole. Recognizing shared responsibility is crucial for developing an ethical framework that holds all parties accountable for AI outcomes.

To create a more just and ethical AI landscape, we must push for stronger regulatory frameworks at both national and international levels. Policymakers have a chance to set standards that enhance accountability and transparency in AI. These regulations should highlight the ethical implications of AI technologies, ensuring that societal values are woven into the development process. By doing this, we can create a regulatory setting that encourages innovation while prioritizing the welfare of individuals and communities.

In addition to regulations, educational efforts that raise awareness of AI ethics are crucial for shaping public discussions. As AI continues to influence many aspects of our lives, it's important to help individuals understand its implications. From schools to community organizations, we should work to educate people about the potential risks of AI and the significance of accountability and transparency. An informed public can advocate for ethical practices, pushing for policies that align with their values and interests.

Ultimately, building a future where AI benefits everyone requires a shared commitment to accountability and transparency. By creating an environment that prioritizes ethical considerations, we can ensure AI systems are designed and implemented with humanity's best interests at heart. The responsibility lies with all of us—developers, companies, policymakers, and citizens—to foster a technological landscape that champions fairness, equity, and justice.

As we tackle the challenges posed by AI, we should seize the chance to redefine our relationship with technology. By holding ourselves and each other accountable, we can unlock the transformative power of AI to uplift society instead of reinforcing existing inequalities. Together, we can champion a future where accountability and transparency are not just ideals but guiding principles shaping the development of artificial intelligence. This journey requires vigilance, advocacy, and a shared vision for a more inclusive and equitable digital world.

Moral Responsibility: Addressing AI-Induced Inequalities

The rise of artificial intelligence has opened up incredible possibilities in technology, promising to transform industries, simplify processes, and improve our daily lives. However, with these exciting advancements comes a significant concern: the risk that AI can make existing social inequalities worse and introduce new forms of discrimination. As AI takes a bigger role in key areas of our lives—from job hiring and loan approvals to policing and healthcare—the ethical duties of technologists and policymakers become increasingly vital. We can't just view AI-induced inequalities as challenges to overcome; we must see them as a moral obligation that requires everyone's involvement to address.

At the center of this conversation are the ethical ideas from philosophers like John Rawls and Immanuel Kant, whose thoughts can guide us toward fairer practices in AI. In his influential book "A Theory of Justice," Rawls talks about the "original position" and the "veil of ignorance." He suggests that when we think about building a fair society, we should do so without knowing our own personal situations. This way, we can make choices that truly prioritize fairness and equality. Applying this idea to AI development means that technologists need to think about how their algorithms will affect everyone, no matter their background. Can we honestly say we're being ethical if we design systems without considering who might get left out?

Kant's view on ethics, particularly his idea of the categorical imperative, also plays a crucial role here. He emphasizes that we should treat individuals as ends in themselves rather than merely as tools to achieve other goals. This concept is deeply connected to the need for AI systems to respect everyone's dignity and rights. When developers create algorithms that unintentionally reinforce biases, they often view people just as data points, sacrificing their humanity for the sake of efficiency or profit. The moral duty of those working with AI isn't just to avoid causing harm; they should actively work toward fairness and justice for all.

The ethical issues surrounding AI-induced inequalities go beyond isolated cases. If we ignore these disparities, they can undermine trust in technology and lead to social unrest. People become skeptical of AI when they feel it doesn't consider their needs or interests. This skepticism can snowball into rejecting technology altogether, stifling growth and innovation. It's important to recognize that neglecting AI bias is not just a moral failure; it poses a risk to society that can create divisions and provoke backlash against technology itself.

To tackle these potential issues, many initiatives and partnerships have emerged, showing a collective effort to confront AI biases. Organizations and coalitions are hard at work to set guidelines for ethical AI use, stressing the need for inclusive design processes that reflect diverse perspectives. For example, the AI for Good Global Summit highlights how technologists, policymakers, and community members can come together to use AI for positive change. By sharing knowledge and collaborating, these groups aim to develop AI systems that are fair and beneficial for everyone.

One standout initiative is the Partnership on AI, which brings together a mix of stakeholders—academics, civil rights advocates, and tech companies—to promote best practices and ethical standards in AI development. This partnership focuses on ongoing dialogue about the challenges posed by AI, ensuring that ethics and responsibility remain a priority in tech development. Through teamwork, these diverse voices can challenge biases and work towards a fairer technological landscape.

Emphasizing inclusivity in AI design is vital. When decisions about technology are made without input from a variety of voices, especially those from underrepresented communities, the risk of bias increases. Inclusive design processes help us understand the needs, concerns, and challenges of different groups. By involving people from diverse backgrounds, technologists can spot potential issues early and create AI systems that cater to a wider range of human experiences. This isn't just about doing the right thing; it's a practical necessity if we want to build systems that serve everyone fairly.

Moreover, promoting transparency in AI development is key to addressing inequalities. Transparency helps everyone understand how decisions are made, enabling them to hold companies accountable. This goes beyond just showing how algorithms work; it includes the need for organizations to reveal the data sources, biases, and assumptions that shape AI systems. When the workings of AI remain hidden, marginalized groups are left exposed to the effects of biased algorithms without any way to respond. Advocating for transparency empowers individuals to demand accountability and challenge unfair practices.

The consequences of ignoring AI bias also affect trust—both in technology and in our institutions. When people face discrimination or injustice through an AI system, their confidence in that technology—and the organizations behind it—declines. Trust isn't something we can take for granted; it must be built and nurtured through responsible actions. When communities feel let down by technology, they might disengage, missing out on innovations that could improve their lives. This disengagement has serious consequences, not just for those affected, but for society as a whole.

Take the example of predictive policing algorithms, which have been criticized for unfairly targeting communities of color. When these systems reinforce existing biases, they not only continue systemic inequalities but also harm the relationship between law enforcement and the communities they're supposed to serve. This breakdown is damaging for social unity and the effectiveness of policing. A lack of trust in our systems can increase tensions and conflicts, ultimately destabilizing the very foundations of society.

Given these ethical challenges, it's clear that the responsibility to address AI-induced inequalities doesn't fall solely on technologists. Policymakers, businesses, and civil society all play essential roles in creating an environment where ethical considerations come first. By implementing strong regulatory frameworks that promote accountability and transparency, governments can set the standard for ethical AI development. This shared responsibility is crucial to ensure that AI technologies reflect our societal values and uphold fairness and justice.

One promising way to encourage responsible AI practices is through interdisciplinary collaboration. By pulling together experts from different fields—such as ethicists, technologists, sociologists, and legal scholars—we can gain a complete understanding of the challenges posed by AI and develop holistic solutions. These interdisciplinary teams can uncover biases in algorithms and brainstorm new ways to weave ethical considerations into technology development. This collaborative approach breaks down barriers, fueling creativity and innovation while keeping the needs of all members of society at the forefront.

Education is another key factor in shaping the ethical landscape surrounding AI. Raising awareness about the implications of AI and promoting ethical understanding can empower individuals to engage thoughtfully with the technology that influences their lives. Educational initiatives can introduce concepts of bias, responsibility, and ethical decision-making to young learners, equipping them with the tools they need to navigate an increasingly complex technological world. As awareness grows, so does the potential for informed advocacy and collective efforts to address injustices embedded in AI systems.

The urgency for responsible action is clear. As AI continues to infiltrate every aspect of our lives, we must keep ethical considerations at the forefront of our conversations. Ignoring this responsibility could have far-reaching, harmful effects, impacting not just individuals but the very fabric of our society. We have a chance to create a future where technology acts as a force for good, promoting fairness and justice instead of deepening existing inequalities.

As we navigate the fast-changing world of artificial intelligence, we must remember that the choices we make today will shape tomorrow's world. By prioritizing moral responsibility and tackling AI-induced inequalities, we can set the stage for a future where technology uplifts everyone. In this effort, technologists, policymakers, and citizens alike need to recognize their shared duty to advocate for ethical practices, encourage inclusivity, and demand accountability from those who control AI.

Ultimately, the moral obligation to address AI biases and inequalities is unmistakable. By nurturing a culture of responsibility, inclusivity, and transparency, we can ensure that advances in artificial intelligence uplift and empower every person, paving the way for a fairer and more just society. In this pursuit, we must remain dedicated to ethical practices, embracing the idea that technology should be a tool for good—one that reflects our shared values and dreams for a better world.

Chapter 9: Imagining the Future: Scenarios of Computational Capitalism

Utopian vs. Dystopian Futures

The rapid growth of artificial intelligence (AI) is changing our society in big ways, creating a world filled with sharp contrasts. On one hand, AI has the potential to bring amazing benefits, offering tools that can boost our abilities, simplify tasks, and close gaps that have existed for a long time in many areas. But on the other hand, there's a more troubling side. If we don't regulate and manage these technologies properly, we could end up facing levels of inequality and division that we've never seen before. These two very different futures—utopian and dystopian—aren't just ideas for a science fiction story; they could become our reality based on the decisions we make today about how to govern AI.

When we think of "utopia," we often picture a place of harmony, progress, and a community where everyone flourishes. In the context of AI governance, a utopian future represents a world where artificial intelligence helps everyone thrive. Imagine a society where universal basic income (UBI) programs, supported by wealth generated through AI, free people from the burden of financial worry. Individuals could follow their dreams, dive into creative projects, and take part in meaningful work without the constant stress of making ends meet. Healthcare, powered by smart algorithms, would offer personalized and preventive care, improving health for everyone. Education would be available to all, with flexible learning systems adjusted to fit each student's unique needs, promoting growth regardless of their background. This is a vision where AI not only enhances our abilities but also respects dignity, inclusivity, and community spirit.

On the flip side, the dystopian future shows a grim picture of a world ruled by AI monopolies. Here, wealth is piled up in the hands of a few, while most people struggle with job losses and the fallout from automation. Instead of improving lives, technology becomes a tool for discrimination, with biases in AI systems worsening existing inequalities. Privacy becomes a thing of the past, with people constantly monitored, their freedom sacrificed for the sake of efficiency and control. Authoritarian regimes take hold, as powerful groups use advanced technologies to maintain control through fear and manipulation. In this bleak scenario, society splits further apart, eroding trust and compassion, leaving many feeling isolated and powerless.

As we explore this complex landscape, it's vital to look at real-world examples and trends that show the path we might take. Take countries like Finland, which have tested equitable AI governance models, including UBI trials. Here, AI has been used to improve resource distribution and streamline processes, proving that UBI is possible and fostering a sense of community that encourages collaboration and innovation. In stark contrast, we can look at areas where AI has been deployed carelessly, without rules or ethical guidelines. In these places, communities have faced serious issues, from job losses to violations of civil liberties, highlighting how a lack of governance can lead to chaos.

The frameworks we create for AI governance will ultimately decide which future we experience. Decentralized governance models, where local communities have a say in shaping AI policies, contrast sharply with centralized control that favors the elite. In a decentralized system, a variety of voices are heard, making sure that AI deployment aligns with shared values and goals. This inclusive approach can lead to transparent systems that hold companies accountable, preventing the misuse of technology. On the other hand, when power is concentrated among a small group, the danger of exploitation rises significantly. Decisions made in boardrooms can have serious consequences, resulting in a society where the wealthy continue to prosper while the less fortunate struggle.

As we think about the future of AI, we must understand that we are not just bystanders in this story; we are active players. The choices we make today regarding AI governance will set the course for our society for years to come. Those who envision a utopian future need to come together to ensure that AI tools are used to promote fairness, inclusion, and the well-being of society, pushing back against any pull toward a dystopian reality. Only through collective effort and a focus on ethical choices can we aim to create a future where technology benefits humanity, rather than the other way around.

This contrast between potential futures reminds us of the weight of responsibility we carry. Each decision, policy, and innovation matters, affecting not just our current lives but also the future health of our society. The struggle between utopia and dystopia is real, encouraging us to engage in conversations about AI governance, challenge the current situation, and fight for systems that prioritize the common good. As we consider the effects of computational capitalism, it becomes clear that the future is still in our hands, and it's our responsibility to write a story that supports fairness and justice in this age of AI.

The Harmonious Society

In the middle of a lively city, sunlight poured through the big windows of a modern apartment, highlighting the bright colors of a small urban garden. On this sunny morning, Mia woke up to the soft chirping of birds, a delightful sound created by her home's AI system, which mixed nature's melody with her favorite morning songs. As she stretched and got ready for her day, the lack of a blaring alarm clock felt refreshing. Instead, her AI friend, Ava, had worked out a wake-up routine that matched her natural sleep cycle, making sure she woke up feeling energized and ready to tackle whatever lay ahead.

Mia lived in a world where artificial intelligence was more like a helpful friend than a bothersome presence. The city she loved had chosen a way of governing that focused on the happiness and health of its people, using AI to improve education, healthcare, and work-life balance. The streets buzzed with laughter and friendly chats as families strolled along, enjoying the walkable paths, lush parks, and community gardens that thrived thanks to smart technology. The air was fresh, and the city sparkled with new ideas, where technology didn't overshadow humanity but instead brought it to life.

After a relaxing breakfast of fresh fruit, oatmeal, and a steaming cup of herbal tea—thanks to Ava's help—Mia settled down at her dining table, which doubled as her workspace. She opened her laptop, powered by a sustainable energy grid managed by AI, and logged into her online learning platform. Education in her society had changed dramatically, moving away from a one-size-fits-all approach to a more personalized experience that recognized each student's strengths and challenges. Mia was studying environmental science, and her courses aimed to not just provide knowledge but also to encourage critical thinking and creativity.

AI was a key player in this educational transformation. It offered real-time feedback, adjusting her coursework to fit her changing interests. Her online classes were interactive and engaging, featuring virtual simulations that let her conduct experiments in ecosystems from around the world without leaving her home. Today, she was involved in a climate change simulation, collaborating with classmates from various countries, each bringing their unique insights shaped by their own backgrounds.

As discussions flowed about possible solutions to environmental issues, Mia felt inspired. The AI made sure everyone's voice was heard, helping them brainstorm solutions that combined scientific data with cultural perspectives. This beautiful mix of technology and humanity was a sign of a society that valued teamwork over competition.

By midday, Mia felt a great sense of achievement. Her flexible schedule allowed her to balance her studies with her love for art. She planned to spend part of the afternoon painting at the community art studio, supported by city resources managed by AI. The studio was filled with modern tools that allowed artists to experiment with different mediums—from digital designs to traditional painting—and also hosted workshops led by talented local artists.

As she walked to the studio, Mia admired her surroundings. The streets were alive with murals and installations created by community members, showcasing their shared creativity. Public art wasn't just for decoration; it was a vital piece of the city's identity, made possible by AI's ability to understand community interests and fund projects that resonated with the residents. This society celebrated the arts, realizing that creativity played a crucial role in emotional health and bringing the community together.

At the studio, Mia immersed herself in the flow of brush strokes and colors. The atmosphere buzzed with inspiration as artists gathered, exchanging tips and ideas. Here, AI played a supporting role, suggesting collaborative projects based on individual styles and interests, creating a sense of community among the creators. Mia found herself teaming up with two other artists—one who focused on digital media and another who worked with sculpture. Together, they imagined an installation that would explore the relationship between technology and nature, highlighting the importance of sustainability.

As the sun began to set, Mia returned home, feeling grateful for her life. The evening was about to unfold into a family dinner—a weekly tradition that brought them together despite their busy schedules. Her parents, both healthcare professionals, shared stories about how AI had transformed patient care, allowing them to focus more on personalized treatments instead of paperwork. With predictive algorithms, they could identify health trends in their community, leading to proactive measures that improved everyone's well-being.

Dinner that night was filled with joy. Laughter echoed through the apartment as they shared stories about their day, each member contributing tales that painted a lively picture of their lives. AI had helped create this warmth and connection, offering meal suggestions based on their nutritional needs and personal tastes, ensuring they nourished their bodies as well as their hearts.

After the dishes were cleared and the table became a space for board games and conversation, Mia leaned back in her chair, taking a moment to appreciate the world around her. She lived in a place that had embraced the potential of AI not as a substitute for human connection but as a way to enhance it. The night ended with a shared sense of purpose, with each family member committed to enriching their community and advocating for a future that valued teamwork and cooperation.

In the days that followed, Mia attended a town hall meeting where residents came together to discuss upcoming community projects. The meeting was supported by AI tools that ensured clarity and inclusivity, allowing everyone to voice their opinions and participate in important discussions. They talked about plans for a new park that would use green technology and an initiative to promote local food sustainability through community gardens.

Mia was moved by the energy in the room. People were excited and passionate, eager to shape their surroundings. The AI systems helped organize decision-making and provided data on community needs, but it was the human spirit—full of creativity, kindness, and determination—that truly guided their actions. The harmony between technology and humanity was clear, reminding them that they were not just passive participants in a system but active creators of their future.

As the sun set that evening, casting a warm glow over the city, Mia felt a strong sense of connection. She was part of something bigger, a society that thrived on collaboration, innovation, and the understanding that technology could be a positive force. This was a vision of the future where people were empowered, free from fear or isolation; where creativity and compassion flourished alongside advancements in artificial intelligence. It was a harmonious society that valued every individual's contribution, reminding Mia that the future was bright and filled with the possibilities of a world fueled by the best of humanity and the transformative power of AI.

Strategic Forecasting: Anticipating Long-Term Societal Shifts

In our fast-paced world, where technology is advancing at lightning speed, it's more important than ever to think ahead about how artificial intelligence (AI) will affect our society. Right now, we're standing at a crossroads of innovation and ethical responsibility. Strategic forecasting is a crucial skill that helps us navigate the complicated impacts of AI. This isn't about gazing into a crystal ball; instead, it's about finding a clear way to look at the possible futures shaped by the choices we make today. To help us in this journey, methods like scenario planning, the Delphi method, and trend analysis are great tools that empower us to plan ahead.

Scenario planning encourages organizations to think about various possible futures. It's an opportunity to imagine the different paths AI could create in our society. This approach isn't just about guesswork; it involves carefully examining trends, uncertainties, and key factors that might shape the way AI evolves. A notable example of this is Shell Oil Company, which used scenario planning in the 1970s to navigate the unpredictable oil market. By developing a range of scenarios, they became better prepared for surprises, leading to strong strategic choices. Similarly, governments around the world are applying this method to get ready for challenges from new technologies. For instance, the Dutch government took part in thorough scenario planning to understand how AI could impact jobs, allowing them to develop policies that not only address job losses but also create new opportunities.

The Delphi method is another important approach, tapping into the expertise of various specialists to build a shared understanding of future trends. By gathering anonymous insights from experts in technology, sociology, and ethics, this method allows us to refine our ideas and predictions. Originally used by the RAND Corporation after WWII to forecast military needs, today it plays a critical role in discussions about AI regulation. For example, the European Commission's High-Level Expert Group on Artificial Intelligence employed the Delphi method to shape guidelines for trustworthy AI, showing how collaboration can help us build a future that respects safety and human rights.

Trend analysis is also a key part of strategic forecasting. It involves looking at current data to spot emerging patterns that might indicate changes in societal attitudes toward AI. This method is especially helpful in gauging public opinion, which can have a significant impact on policy decisions. As AI continues to influence our daily lives, monitoring shifts in public sentiment—whether it's fear about job losses or excitement for AI's potential to address major global issues—becomes crucial. For example, the Pew Research Center conducts surveys to understand how the public views AI, providing valuable insights that can guide both policymakers and tech developers. By keeping an eye on these trends, stakeholders can make informed choices that align with the community's values and expectations.

While we explore forecasting, it's vital to pinpoint key indicators that show whether we're heading toward a bright or troubling future. In the realm of AI, there are several important factors to keep in mind. The growth of AI ethics is at the forefront, as ongoing talks about the moral implications of AI technologies shape public and government discussions. Changes in legislation concerning AI regulation can also reflect society's readiness to embrace or resist these new technologies. Establishing frameworks that focus on accountability and transparency will be crucial in guiding us toward a future where technology benefits everyone.

Public sentiment is a powerful influence in this equation. As people become more aware of the ethical issues surrounding AI, like data privacy and bias in algorithms, it highlights a growing social consciousness that demands responsible innovation. Grassroots movements advocating for ethical AI practices are rising, indicating a shift toward a more informed and engaged public. For instance, organizations like the Algorithmic Justice League are working hard to address bias in AI systems, fostering discussions that aim for fair outcomes for everyone. Keeping track of such movements can provide great insights into the societal landscape, helping us respond strategically to emerging challenges.

Additionally, we can't overlook the impact of AI on employment. The ongoing discussion about job displacement versus new job creation is a critical factor in predicting how AI will shape our future. By observing trends in vocational training and reskilling efforts, we can understand how society is responding to the changing job landscape. Companies that focus on workforce development and invest in education aligned with emerging technologies will be in a stronger position to succeed in an AI-driven economy. Policymakers need to stay alert, crafting laws that help with this transition while also protecting workers who might be adversely affected by automation.

However, predicting the future is not something we can do alone. It's essential to involve a diverse range of stakeholders to gain a well-rounded understanding of AI's possible effects. Conversations about AI governance should include voices from various sectors—community members, technologists, policymakers, and ethicists—so we can work together to create visions for the future. Collaborative efforts foster open dialogue and build consensus, ensuring that the policies we create reflect the needs and values of all members of society.

Initiatives to encourage stakeholder engagement are already happening in many communities. Hackathons and public forums provide spaces for citizens to share their ideas and concerns about AI technologies. For example, in San Francisco, city leaders have started a series of community workshops to explore how AI will affect urban life, directly involving residents in the decision-making process. Such efforts not only empower individuals but also create a sense of ownership over the future of AI in our society.

Building visions for the future together helps us tap into the creativity and wisdom of the community. By welcoming different perspectives, we can challenge assumptions and find innovative solutions to the issues that AI presents. The potential for productive discussions among stakeholders is vast, and it's here that we can discover the seeds of change that lead to a more fair and inclusive future.

As we look forward, it's crucial that we rally together for action. Instead of being passive observers of technological change, we should strive to advocate for a future where AI serves the greater good. This advocacy goes beyond just being aware; it means actively participating in shaping the policies and frameworks that will govern how AI technologies are used. Each of us has a role in influencing the direction of AI in our society, whether through community involvement, promoting ethical practices, or pushing for responsible legislation.

The responsibility of our generation is significant. The choices we make today will have lasting effects, impacting not just our lives, but also the lives of countless others in the future. We are at a pivotal moment, and the ability to create a promising future rests in our hands. It's our duty to ensure that technology doesn't reflect societal inequalities but acts as a bridge that connects and uplifts everyone.

Let's seize this chance to build a culture of teamwork and innovation that mirrors our shared values. By actively taking part in discussions about AI governance, we can create an environment where technology enhances human potential, rather than takes away from it. The stories we create today will shape the narratives of tomorrow, and it's up to us to make sure these stories are filled with hope, inclusion, and the promise of a brighter future.

As we navigate the complexities of an AI-driven world, we need to stay alert and adaptable. The landscape will continue to change, bringing new challenges and opportunities our way. However, equipped with strategic forecasting methods and a commitment to engaging diverse stakeholders, we can face these uncertainties with confidence and clarity. We can chart a path that not only anticipates change but also embraces it with open arms.

In the end, the future isn't predetermined; it's a canvas where we can paint our collective hopes and dreams. Together, we can create a society where technology acts as an ally, helping us tackle the pressing issues of our time while fostering connection, creativity, and compassion. As we peer into the future, let's remember that the power to shape our world lies not with a few, but within all of us. The time to take action is now, and together we can carve out a path to a future that honors our shared humanity and celebrates the best that technology has to offer.

Chapter 10: Pathways to an Equitable AI Future

Policy Recommendations

Artificial intelligence has quickly become a major part of our daily lives, influencing everything from how we work to how we connect with others and even how we see ourselves. However, as we've discussed throughout this book, the rise of AI has also uncovered serious inequalities, making social disparities even worse, much like those seen during the Gilded Age. As we reach this pivotal moment in technological change, we need to tackle these inequalities directly. Creating a fair AI future isn't just about recognizing the problems; it's about making real changes through smart policy decisions.

Regulatory frameworks are key to shaping how AI gets developed and used. Without clear rules and regulations, the risk of worsening inequalities grows significantly. Think about the consequences of AI systems trained on biased data. If left unchecked, these systems can reinforce stereotypes and deepen existing biases, especially against marginalized groups. To prevent this, policymakers need to focus on developing strong regulatory measures that promote accountability and transparency in AI systems.

A vital first step in this effort is creating a thorough framework to evaluate the ethical implications of AI technologies. This framework should set clear guidelines for how data is collected and used, ensuring diverse datasets are employed to train AI models and help prevent systemic biases. Additionally, regular audits of AI systems should be required so that any discriminatory outcomes can be identified and corrected. An independent oversight body could be formed to monitor these systems, making sure they follow ethical standards that support fairness and justice.

Public involvement is also a fundamental part of successful policymaking in the AI space. It's not enough to just create laws from the top down; we need to hear from the communities most affected by AI technologies. Organizing public forums, workshops, and discussions can provide a platform for citizens to voice their concerns and hopes regarding AI. By encouraging open dialogue, policymakers can gain a better understanding of the diverse effects of AI on different groups, leading to policies that genuinely meet the needs of society.

The importance of international cooperation can't be stressed enough. In a world where technology knows no borders, countries must work together to create a unified approach to AI governance. By collaborating, nations can establish shared ethical standards for AI development, which will help prevent a scenario where companies prioritize profits over ethics. Furthermore, international organizations like the United Nations can help facilitate conversations about global AI policies, fostering a sense of responsibility among nations to prioritize equity.

Training and education are crucial for promoting fairness in AI as well. Policymakers should support educational programs designed to give people the skills needed to engage in the AI revolution. This includes incorporating AI literacy into school curricula from a young age. By creating an environment where everyone—regardless of their economic background—can learn about AI, we can achieve a more balanced representation in the tech workforce. This diversity in perspectives will help reduce bias and ensure better outcomes for everyone.

In addition to educational efforts, it's vital to support entrepreneurship in underrepresented communities. Establishing funding opportunities for startups led by individuals from marginalized backgrounds can spark innovation and ensure diverse voices are part of the AI conversation. This support could take the form of grants, mentorship programs, or partnerships with established tech companies looking to broaden their investments.

Finally, as we think about the future of AI, we must not forget the importance of social safety nets in our policy recommendations. With the rise of AI, many jobs could be lost, creating serious challenges for workers in various sectors. Policymakers should enhance social safety nets to protect those most vulnerable to job loss. This might include retraining programs, unemployment benefits, and support systems to help individuals transition into new careers. By investing in our workforce, we can ensure that people are prepared for the changes AI brings and are empowered to thrive in this fast-evolving environment.

As we look ahead, these policy recommendations shouldn't be seen as standalone solutions but as interconnected strategies that together can lead us to a fair AI future. When stakeholders across different sectors begin to explore these approaches, the aim of making AI technology accessible to everyone becomes more attainable. It's not just about being aware of the challenges; it's about actively participating in creating a future where the benefits of artificial intelligence are available to all, not just a privileged few.

Building an equitable AI future requires courage and teamwork from all parts of society. Technology companies, government bodies, and community organizations must unite to push for fair practices. Accepting this responsibility means understanding not only the potential of AI to improve lives but also the obligation to make sure its benefits reach everyone. By cultivating an ethical and inclusive approach to AI governance, we can reduce inequalities and avoid repeating the errors of the past.

As we navigate this complex terrain, let's remember that the true power for transformative change lies not only in the algorithms themselves but in the values they represent, the data they process, and most importantly, the people they serve. A future where AI is used for social good is possible, but we need to take deliberate steps to ensure it is founded on principles of fairness, equity, and inclusion. This is a journey we all share, and it's up to each one of us to steer toward a future where technology uplifts rather than divides.

Inclusive Technological Development

Artificial intelligence has the power to change our lives for the better, making things more efficient, boosting productivity, and opening up exciting new possibilities.

However, as we stand on the edge of this technological change, it's crucial to think about who is involved in creating these innovative tools and who will actually benefit from them. The current world of AI development isn't just shaped by new technology; it's also influenced by the significant gaps that exist among different communities. These gaps show up in many ways, such as systemic biases, unequal access to education, and economic challenges. We need to tackle these obstacles directly if we want to build a truly inclusive and fair technological future.

One big issue in the AI field is the lack of diverse voices in the tech industry. The stories and ideas that drive AI development often come from a small group of similar individuals. This lack of diversity can lead to misunderstandings about the needs and experiences of marginalized communities. For example, facial recognition technology has faced significant backlash for its inaccuracies when identifying people with darker skin tones. This isn't just a technical issue; it highlights the importance of having diverse perspectives during the design and development stages. We need to push for an environment that actively includes voices from all backgrounds, especially those who have been left out of the tech conversation in the past.

Education is a key part of making things inclusive, serving as a bridge to greater access and participation. Unfortunately, we know that not everyone has equal access to quality education, often depending on their socio-economic status. For underrepresented groups, this lack of opportunity can feel like an overwhelming barrier that keeps them from pursuing careers in AI and tech. That's why we need to prioritize efforts that promote education and training in AI-related fields. Providing scholarships for individuals from marginalized communities can help to provide opportunities where there were none. Additionally, mentorship programs that connect students with professionals in the field can offer guidance and support, helping them feel welcomed in an industry that can often feel exclusive.

Looking at successful initiatives, partnerships between tech companies and educational institutions can serve as a strong example of how to promote inclusive technological development. These collaborations can create tailored programs that equip students with the skills they need to succeed in the AI landscape. Imagine coding boot camps and AI training workshops happening in underprivileged neighborhoods, encouraging individuals to explore these fields. By making AI education more accessible, we can open the door for a more diverse workforce that truly reflects the society it serves.

Another way to encourage inclusivity in tech development is through participatory design processes. This approach focuses on working with end-users right from the beginning, making sure the technology created truly meets their needs. By actively involving marginalized communities in the creation of AI tools, we can ensure their perspectives are valued and their needs are met. This not only leads to better solutions but also gives participants a sense of ownership, empowering them to be co-creators rather than just consumers of technology.

We can't overlook the importance of ethical AI practices in our mission for inclusivity. As we develop guidelines to maintain fairness, accountability, and transparency, these principles should be at the heart of AI development. Organizations need to embrace ethical frameworks that prioritize fair outcomes and involve diverse stakeholders in their design. Ethical considerations shouldn't be an afterthought or just something to check off a list; they need to be integrated into every step of the technological development process. This can include regular audits of AI systems to spot and fix potential biases and discriminatory practices. An independent oversight body could play a key role in keeping things accountable and ensuring that ethical standards support all community members.

Real change often comes from those working on the front lines. By sharing interviews and personal stories from diverse tech practitioners, we can highlight the real benefits of inclusivity in technology development. These narratives remind us of the powerful impact that different perspectives can have on innovation. For instance, think about a team of engineers working together to create a healthcare AI tool. By bringing together individuals from different backgrounds—like healthcare professionals and community advocates—they can develop a product that is not only technically advanced but also culturally sensitive and relevant to the populations it aims to help. Their varied experiences and insights help them understand the challenges different communities face, leading to solutions that genuinely address their needs.

Representation isn't just about who works at tech companies; it also includes the stories that surround AI. The narratives we share about technology shape how we all perceive its potential and limitations. By focusing on the voices of those who have historically been left out, we can create a deeper, more meaningful dialogue about the impact of AI on society. The stories from individuals with diverse backgrounds can inspire future generations to enter the field while ensuring that the narratives we share reflect the realities of a complex world.

Moreover, efforts to promote diversity and inclusion should not be fleeting or superficial; they need to aim for sustainability. This means making long-term commitments from tech companies, educational institutions, and policymakers to build an ecosystem that nurtures diverse talent. It's not enough to simply hire a few individuals from underrepresented backgrounds; we must create an environment where they can thrive, grow, and take on leadership roles. This can be done through ongoing training, support networks, and opportunities for advancement.

In the end, creating an inclusive landscape for technological development is not just the right thing to do; it's also crucial for our economy. Research consistently shows that diverse teams perform better than those that are homogenous. By tapping into the collective intelligence and creativity of individuals from various backgrounds, we can spark innovation, enhance problem-solving, and boost overall productivity. As we move forward, we need to embrace the diversity of thought, experience, and perspective within our communities.

The journey to an equitable AI future is lit up by our dedication to inclusivity in tech development. By tackling the barriers that keep diverse voices from participating, supporting education and mentorship, and weaving ethical practices into our approaches, we can create a technological landscape that reflects our society and meets its needs. By fostering an environment that celebrates diversity in all its forms, we'll not only improve the quality of technological solutions but also build a sense of belonging and empowerment in our communities.

As we work towards inclusivity, let's remember that the future of AI—just like the future of society—should be guided by principles of fairness, equity, and shared responsibility. Each of us has a role to play in this vision, to challenge the status quo, and to ensure that as we advance in technology, we do so in a way that uplifts and includes everyone. The stakes are high, and it's our responsibility to make sure that today's technological advancements lead to a more just and equitable tomorrow.

Building Resilient Societies

As our society shifts and changes with the rise of artificial intelligence, one thing stands out: creating strong, resilient communities is more important than ever. Resilience, in this case, means a community's ability to handle and adapt to various challenges—whether they come from changes in the economy, social issues, or technological advancements. In a world where AI is reshaping jobs and industries, thinking about how we can make our communities more resilient is key to ensuring that everyone benefits from these changes, rather than leaving some people behind.

Throughout history, communities have shown an incredible ability to bounce back, especially during tough times. For example, when economic crises hit, we often see grassroots movements popping up. These movements are fueled by people who refuse to let their livelihoods slip away without a fight. They come together, sharing resources and knowledge, and supporting each other in creative ways. This spirit of togetherness isn't just inspiring; it's vital for survival. By nurturing collaboration and support, communities can better face the challenges brought on by AI.

One effective way to build resilience is by setting up cooperative platforms. These groups, usually started by local community members, focus on shared ownership and mutual benefits instead of just making profits. Picture a neighborhood where local shops join forces to create a cooperative grocery store. This not only provides fresh food and necessary items but also creates jobs, boosts the local economy, and strengthens the bond among residents. In this scenario, the community takes control of its economic future, creating a safeguard against the unpredictable shifts of the broader market.

Another exciting way to enhance community resilience is through community-owned AI projects. As AI technology grows, it's essential for local communities to have a voice in the conversation. Imagine a small town where residents team up with tech developers to design AI tools that address their specific challenges. These tools could range from smart farming solutions to improved public services. By actively participating in the tech development process, communities can ensure the tools they use meet their needs and give them a sense of empowerment.

Local innovation hubs also play a key role in building resilience. These hubs provide a space for new ideas to flourish, offering resources for community members to experiment and grow. They can host workshops on the latest technologies, mentor new entrepreneurs, and connect people with resources that might otherwise feel out of reach. By encouraging collaboration among different groups, these hubs can spark creativity and motivate people to think differently about solving local challenges. In uncertain times, these hubs become safe havens for innovation and support.

However, fostering community resilience goes beyond creating cooperatives, community-led initiatives, and innovation hubs. It calls for a comprehensive approach that understands the need for social safety nets. As AI continues to change the job market, strong safety nets become even more critical. Universal basic income (UBI) is one such idea that can provide financial stability for individuals during transitions. The concept is straightforward but impactful: by guaranteeing a basic income, we can help cushion the financial blows that come with job losses due to technological changes.

Think about a factory town dealing with automation. As machines take over jobs, many workers find themselves in limbo about their futures. Introducing UBI in this situation can offer a safety net, allowing individuals the freedom to retrain for new jobs without the constant worry of financial disaster. This security can motivate people to pursue training and education that align with the skills needed in an ever-changing job landscape.

Retraining programs are another important part of strong social safety nets. As industries transform, workers may discover that their skills no longer fit the demands of the job market. By investing in thorough retraining programs, communities can help displaced workers learn new skills that match emerging opportunities. These programs could range from coding boot camps to vocational training in promising fields like renewable energy or healthcare.

Looking back at the history of social reform can teach us valuable lessons here. For instance, during the New Deal in the United States, various programs were set up to revive the economy during the Great Depression. These efforts not only eased immediate hardships but also laid the groundwork for future economic growth. By examining historical examples, we can understand how proactive steps can help lessen the impact of rapid changes.

Additionally, as we reflect on how AI affects mental health and well-being, it's clear that a resilient society must prioritize support systems to tackle these challenges. The emotional strain of job loss, combined with the uncertainty of fast-paced technological advancements, can heavily burden individuals and communities. Supporting mental health initiatives—like community counseling programs and wellness resources—can be crucial in helping people navigate these changes.

Civic engagement is another vital element when it comes to integrating AI into community life. When residents actively participate in decisions that affect them, they can influence the development of technologies that shape their daily lives. This involvement can take many forms, from town hall meetings discussing local AI projects to participatory budgeting where community members decide how to allocate funds for tech-related initiatives.

Looking at examples of successful AI integration into public services can provide inspiration. Some cities have already used AI systems to optimize public transportation routes based on real-time data. By involving community members in these processes, cities can ensure that the solutions are not only efficient but also fair and responsive to the needs of the people. The more engaged residents are in shaping these technologies, the better the outcomes will be for the community.

The idea of creating an inclusive digital public square also plays a crucial role in civic engagement in the context of AI. As digital platforms become the main way we communicate and share information, it's essential that these spaces are open to everyone. This inclusivity means working to bridge the digital divide that affects many communities. By investing in internet access for underserved areas and supporting digital literacy programs, we can empower everyone to participate fully in the digital age.

In working towards a future where AI serves to empower rather than exploit, we must remember that the key to resilience lies in community collaboration. A diverse and engaged population is better prepared to handle the complexities of a technology-driven world. As communities come together to share knowledge, resources, and experiences, they lay the foundation for a future that prioritizes the well-being of all its members.

In the end, building resilient societies in the age of AI requires a multi-pronged approach that emphasizes community involvement, creative solutions, and strong social safety nets. As we witness the rapid evolution of technology, let's remember the strength of our communities in overcoming challenges. By creating an environment where individuals feel empowered to share their thoughts, contribute ideas, and take part in decision-making, we can ensure that the future of AI is one that lifts everyone, rather than leaving anyone behind.